Walk Around

MiG-15 Fagot

By Hans-Heiri Stapfer

Color by Don Greer

Illustrated by David Gebhardt and Darren Glenn

Walk Around Number 40

squadron/signal publications

Introduction

In early November 1950, United Nations fighter pilots over North Korea encountered a formidable, swept-wing high performance fighter, which was quickly identified as the Soviet-built MiG-15. Almost overnight the name 'MiG' became infamous in the West, as F-86 Sabres and MiG-15s clashed over 'MiG Alley.' The MiG-15 was the first jet fighter to be mass-produced by the MiG Design Bureau (named for the two men heading the bureau, Artjom Ivanovich Mikoyan and Mikhail Iosifovich Gurevich), and over the years the name 'MiG' has become virtually synonymous with Soviet fighters.

During early 1947, work on the 'Project S' prototype began at State Aircraft Factory 1 at Kuybyshev. The aircraft was designed as a fast climbing, heavily armed fighter able to intercept American bombers attacking the Soviet Union. The first prototype, 'S-01,' first flew from Zhukovsky airfield (known as Ramenskoye in the West) on 30 December 1947 with Viktor Nikolayevich Yuganov at the controls.

The first production MiG-15 made its maiden flight on 30 December 1948, exactly a year after the first flight of the S-01 prototype. The MiG-15 was powered by the 2,200 kg (4,850 lb) thrust RD-45 turbojet engine, a Soviet-manufactured copy of the Rolls Royce Nene. Once NATO had identified the MiG-15 as an operational fighter, it assigned the Air Standards Coordinating Committee reporting name 'Fagot-A' to the aircraft.

A total of 1,344 MiG-15 Fagot-As were produced between late 1948 and early 1950 by not less than five State Aircraft Factories, when the type was phased out in favor of the improved MiG-15bis 'Fagot-B,' with a more powerful VK-1 engine having a thrust of 2,700 kg (5,950 lb), increased fuel capacity, and enlarged speed brakes. By 1952 no fewer than 7,936 MiG-15bis fighters had been manufactured in the Soviet Union.

The MiG-15 and MiG-15bis also were license-built in Czechoslovakia by the Letov and Aero factories under the designation S-102 (Fagot-A) and S-103 (Fagot-B). A total of 821 S-102s and 620 S-103s were built between 1951 and 1957. In Poland, PZL manufactured 227 MiG-15s (called Lim-1 in Polish Air Force service) and 500 MiG-15bis (known as Lim-2) from 1953 to 1956. In all, over 17,000 MiG-15s of all variants, including the two-seat MiG-15UTI, were produced.

Acknowledgements and Photo Credits

United States Air Force Museum
Armeemuseum der DDR
Dan Antoniu
Bob Bird
Robert Bock
Stephan Boshniakov
Amelia Cachay
Czechoslovak Air Force Museum
Larry Davis
Deutsches Museum - Werft Schleissheim
Nigel A. Eastaway
Gerhard Filchner
Robert Gretzyngier
Ödön Horvath
Zdenek Hurt
Lubomir Kudlicka
Martin Kyburz
Wojciech Luczak
Hans-Joachim Mau
Maxwell Research Center
Dusan Mikolas
Andrzej Morgala
Andras Nagy
Alain Pelletier
George Petkov
George Punka
R.A.R.T.
Tibor Sinka
Chuck Stewart
Wolfgang Tamme
Zdenek Titz
Michal Ovcácík
Hans-Georg Volprich
Jiry Vrany
Nicolas J. Waters III
Simon Watson
4+ Publishing Company
Daniel Bader
Aeromaster Decals/Eagle Strike Productions

ISBN 0-89747-495-3

If you have any photographs of aircraft, armor, soldiers or ships of any nation, particularly wartime snapshots, why not share them with us and help make Squadron/Signal's books all the more interesting and complete in the future? Any photograph sent to us will be copied and the original returned. The donor will be fully credited for any photos used. Please send them to:

Squadron/Signal Publications, Inc.
1115 Crowley Drive
Carrollton, TX 75011-5010

Если у вас есть фотографии самолётов, вооружения, солдат или кораблей любой страны, особенно, снимки времён войны, поделитесь с нами и помогите сделать новые книги издательства Эскадрон/Сигнал ещё интереснее. Мы переснимем ваши фотографии и вернём оригиналы. Имена приславших снимки будут сопровождать все опубликованные фотографии. Пожалуйста, присылайте фотографии по адресу:

Squadron/Signal Publications, Inc.
1115 Crowley Drive
Carrollton, TX 75011-5010

軍用機、装甲車両、兵士、軍艦などの写真を所持しておられる方はいらっしゃいませんか？どの国のものでも結構です。作戦中に撮影されたものが特に良いのです。Squadron/Signal社の出版する刊行物において、このような写真は内容を一層充実し、興味深くすることができます。当方にお送り頂いた写真は、複写の後お返しいたします。出版物中に写真を使用した場合は、必ず提供者のお名前を明記させて頂きます。お写真は下記にご送付ください。

Squadron/Signal Publications, Inc.
1115 Crowley Drive
Carrollton, TX 75011-5010

Front Cover: A Soviet-built MiG-15bis of the Chinese contingent undergoes outdoor maintenance during the Korean War. The Fagot-B received the designation 'J-2' in Chinese service.

Title page: A line up of MiG-15 Fagot-As of the Fortele Aeriene ale Republicii Socialiste Romania (Romanian Air Force) in the late 1950s. The MiG-15 became the most widely used jet fighter in the world, with a total of over 17,000 MiG-15 fighters and trainers built in the Soviet Union, Poland, and Czechoslovakia between 1948 and 1961.

Back Cover: Captain Stepan A. Fedorets of the 913th Fighter Aviation Regiment downs a USAF F-86 Sabre on 12 April 1953. The MiG-15bis, 'Red 93,' belonged to the Soviet contingent flying in support of North Korea. The camouflage of green, brown, and sand was applied in the field. Captain Fedorets claimed a total of seven victories over United Nations aircraft during the course of the Korean War.

The MiG-15 has been called "The aircraft of the soldier." It was indeed a pilot's airplane with outstanding flight characteristics and was easy to maintain, even under the most austere front-line conditions. 'Red 1915' of the Polish Air Force was built by PZL (Panstwowe Zaklady Lotnicze/State Aircraft Factory) at Mielec in Poland. A total of 500 MiG-15bis were license-built in Poland under the designation Lim-2 (Licencyjny Mysliwiec 2 — License Fighter 2).

(Above) A line-up of Romanian Air Force MiG-15bis manufactured by the Aero Vodochody plant in the Ceskoslovenska Socialisticka Republica (Czechoslovak Socialist Republic). The Romanian Air Force used two-, three-, and four-digit tactical numbers on their MiG-15s and MiG-15bis.

(Below) Czechoslovak-built MiG-15bis (S-103) of the 9. Stihaci Letecky Pluk (9th Fighter Regiment) of the Letectvo Ceskoslovenske Lidove Armady (Czechoslovak Air Force) during a winter exercise. All aircraft are equipped with the PTB-260 slipper tanks. At the time a total of nearly 1,000 MiG-15s were operational in 18 Czechoslovak Fighter Regiments.

(Above) 'Black 3244,' a Czechoslovak-built MiG-15bisR (serial number 613244) at Pardubice Air Force Base in 1969. This particular Fagot-B of the Czechoslovak Air Force carries the crest of the city of Ostrava on the nose, a common marking on Fagots belonging to the 30. Sbolp "Ostravsky" (30th Fighter Bomber Regiment). The leading edge of the tail fin is painted blue. The MiG-15bisR — "R" stands for "Razvedchik" (reconnaissance) — carried only a single NR-23 cannon to port. The port inboard cannon was deleted to make room for the AFA-1M vertical camera.

A Romanian pilot climbs into his MiG-15 Fagot-A. The two-piece gun blast panel on the lower part of the nose is a typical feature of the Fagot-A and the early production batches of the MiG-15bis. The S-13 gun camera in the upper air intake lip is slightly offset to starboard.

This Romanian Air Force pilot has just accomplished a mission. 'Red 1129' is a late production MiG-15bis equipped with two NR-23 23 mm cannons as evidenced by the blistered shell ejection ports.

MiG-15 Fagot-As of the Romanian Air Force. The jet fighter nearest the camera is serial number 231767. The last three digits are repeated as a tactical number. The serial number is painted on the upper nose covering, the blisters for the NS-23 KM cannon, and the nose wheel door. The serial number denotes that these MiG-15 Fagot-As were all built in Vodochody, Czechoslovakia, by Aero.

An impressive line-up of MiG-15bis Fagot-Bs of the Chinese People's Liberation Army Air Force, which designated the aircraft 'J-2.' All aircraft carry large red four-digit tactical numbers. The national marking was applied on the rear fuselage as well on the wing upper and lower surface. All Fagot-As and -Bs operated by the Chinese People's Liberation Army Air Force were supplied by the Soviet Union; the production of the J-2 never took place in China.

Food for Chinese Regiments in the Korean conflict was strictly rationed, and many Fagot pilots were chronically malnourished. As a result, they suffered gravity-induced loss of consciousness in high-G maneuvers. This J-2 has received a locally applied camouflage, which was not uncommon for Fagot-Bs assigned to Aviation Regiments fighting over North Korea.

A large Chinese contingent took part in the Korean War against United Nations forces. In the early stages of the conflict, the hastily trained MiG-15 pilots became easy prey for the well-trained American pilots. Many Chinese-operated J-2 Fagot-Bs, like these, received a front line-applied camouflage consisting of mottled green, brown and sand colors.

A Soviet pilot prepares for a mission in his MiG-15bis Fagot-B. The rugged landing gear of the MiG-15 proved ideal for unimproved landing fields. At least 17,312 MiG-15s of all variants were built in the Soviet Union, Poland, and Czechoslovakia.

Albanian Fagot-Bs were built in the Soviet Union and initially delivered to the Chinese Air Force, which added a small access hatch to the port side of the nose. '548,' based at Kucova Air Force Base, carries new markings introduced after the fall of Communism in Albania.

'Red 708,' a MiG-15bis (serial number 31530708) of the 31. Vadaszrepülö Ezred (31st Fighter Wing), Magyar Legierö (Hungarian Air Force). This Fagot-B was delivered to the Hungarian Air Force in December 1952. Hungarian MiG-15s were withdrawn from service in 1975.

(Above) The Al Quwwat al Jawwiya al Aljaza'eriiya (Algerian Air Force) received its first five MiG-15bis in November 1962. The Algerian pilots were instructed by Egyptian personnel at Mers-El-Kebir Air Force Base. A total of 20 Fagot-Bs, all former Egyptian Air Force MiG-15bis, were operated by the Algerian Air Force. In 1963 some Algerian Fagots saw combat during the brief conflict with Morocco.

(Above) MiG-15bis of the 30. Sbolp "Ostravsky" (30th Fighter Bomber Regiment), Czechoslovak Air Force. The first MiG-15bisR in line is painted with a blue tail leading edge. 'Black 3912' has a black fin tip. As a fighter-bomber, the MiG-15 remained operational in the Czechoslovak Air Force until 1984.

(Left) Line-up of MiG-15s of the 30th Fighter Bomber Regiment during 1969. All Fagot-Bs were painted with the crest of the city of Ostrava, although the unit was based at this time at Hradec Kralove (known as Königgrätz in World War II). This highly decorated Czechoslovak Air Force regiment began operations in the Ostrava region during the closing days of World War II with Ilyushin Il-2s.

'White 4115,' a former Chinese Navy J-2 Fagot-B (serial number 1411), was acquired by Combat Jets Inc. of Houston, Texas. The aircraft received the American registration N15MG and belongs today to the EAA Aviation Foundation Inc. at Oshkosh, Wisconsin. The MiG-15bis is active in air shows, usually teamed with an F-86 Sabre.

This beautifully restored MiG-15 (serial number 1411) was assembled at China's Shenyang Factory in 1954 from Soviet-built components and is one of many Fagots now flying in the United States. The registration N15MG has been applied in small characters on the rear fuselage. MiG-15s have been advertised for $35,000, but civilian owners usually have to spend about $100,000 to get a Fagot airborne. Reportedly, the ex-Chinese MiG-15s are of much better fit and finish than the Fagots supplied by former Warsaw Pact countries.

J-2 Fagot-Bs of the Chinese People's Liberation Army Air Force not only saw action over North Korea, but also were frequently engaged with Taiwanese and American aircraft intruding into Chinese airspace during the 1950s.

N15MG, a Chinese-assembled MiG-15bis, previously served with the Chinese Navy.

A Chinese instructor uses models to illustrate tactical maneuvers next to a camouflaged MiG-15bis. In contrast to Soviet pilots who flew in the Korean War, the Chinese had no restrictions placed on them and operated over the entire Korean peninsula.

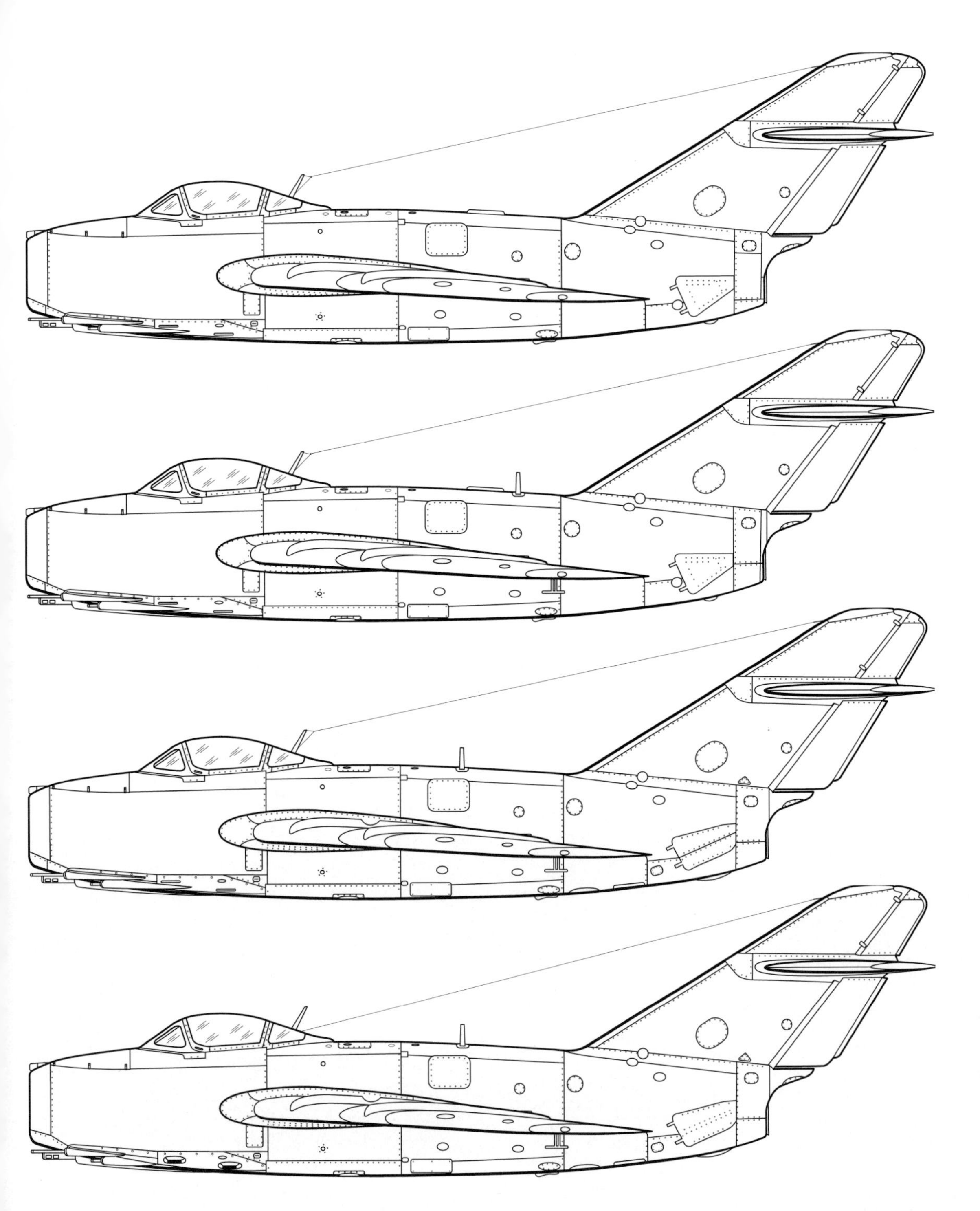

MiG-15 Fagot-A

The MiG-15 Fagot-A was the first production version, having small triangular speed brakes, a dorsal fairing for the antenna of the RPKO-10M radio compass, and a small tail bumper.

MiG-15 Fagot-A (modified)

A number of MiG-15 Fagot-As were fitted with the RV-2 Kristal (Crystal) radio altimeter, with antennas mounted under the inner starboard wing as well the outer port wing tip. Also added was an SRO-1 Bariy-M (Barium-M) IFF transponder with a ventral blade aerial on top of the rear fuselage, just behind the fairing of the radio compass antenna.

MiG-15bis Fagot-B (early)

The MiG-15bis Fagot-B was equipped with larger, rectangular speed brakes and an enlarged tail bumper. On the lower rear fuselage a circular covering for the ARK-5 radio compass and a rectangular avionics bay for the MRP-48 marker beacon receiver were added. The fairing for the RPKO-10M radio compass antenna on top of the rear fuselage was deleted and the starboard mounted EKSR-46 flare launcher relocated.

MiG-15bis Fagot-B (late)

The late production MiG-15bis differed from early Fagot-Bs in having a revised antenna cable leading from the tail directly into the starboard fuselage. The NS-23 KM cannon was replaced by the NR-23 with short fairings and blistered shell ejection ports. The two-piece gun blast panel was replaced by a one-piece panel. The landing light was relocated from the air intake splitter into the starboard side wing, and one-piece speed brakes replaced the two-piece speed brakes of previous models.

This Lim-2 (serial number 1B 012-05) previously flew with the Polskie Wojsko Lotnicze (Polish Air Force) as 'Red 1205.' The Fagot-B was sold in the United States, where the privately owned fighter was registered N205JM. For the TV movie "Steal the Sky," oversized Iraqi Air Force markings were applied.

This MiG-15bis (serial number 2292) was built in 1954 and previously saw service with the Chinese People's Liberation Army Air Force. It was shipped to the United States in January 1992 and registered N90589. The tactical number 'White 1170' as well as the Soviet markings are fictional. The owner of this particular Fagot-B is James K. Wickersham from Danville, California.

This former Polish Air Force Lim-2 was purchased by the Operational Test and Evaluation Office of the Department of Defense. The first exercise with such MiG-15s as "aggressors" was held in fall 1988 at Kirtland AFB, Albuquerque, New Mexico. No national markings were applied during these exercises.

This is a privately owned Lim-2 (serial number 1B-016-29). The Fagot-B received its U.S. registration N629BM in March 1987. It retained its original Polish Air Force four-digit tactical number, 'Red 1629', but false Soviet Air Force markings were applied. This Fagot-B is currently operated by John Macguire of Santa Teresa, New Mexico.

A number of former Magyar Legierö (Hungarian Air Force) MiG-15bis were stored at the Aeroking Dump at Vecses very near the international airport of Budapest in summer 1992. The four-digit code applied on the Fagot-Bs reflects the year the plane was struck off charge.

MiG-15bis 'Red 1978' rests without wings at the Aeroking dump at Vecses. Most of the Aeroking Fagot-Bs had been previously exhibited as 'gate guards' at air bases or as memorials at public places. With the end of Communism, these MiG-15s were quickly removed from their locations.

'Red 1977,' a former Hungarian Air Force MiG-15bis, rests on a mountain of other aircraft parts at the Aeroking dump at Vecses near Budapest. In the meantime, all other aircraft had been removed. Most of the exhibits were either scrapped or taken to other spots in Hungary.

This MiG-15bis (serial number 31530891), 'Red 981,' was one of the few former Hungarian Air Force Fagot-Bs to retain their original tactical numbers upon being phased out of service. This aircraft had been manufactured at Gosudarstvenny Aviatsionny Zavod 31 (State Aircraft Factory 31) at Tbilisi in the Georgian Soviet Socialist Republic.

The MiG-15 Fagot-A had small triangle-shaped speed brakes and a small tail bumper. The fairing on top of the rear fuselage covers the RPKO-10M radio compass. 'Red 02' was one of the few Soviet-built Fagot-As in Polish Air Force service, assigned to the 1. Pulku Lotnictwa Mysliwskiego "Warszawa" (1st Fighter Aviation Regiment "Warsaw") at Minsk-Mazowiecki Air Force Base.

Fuselage Development

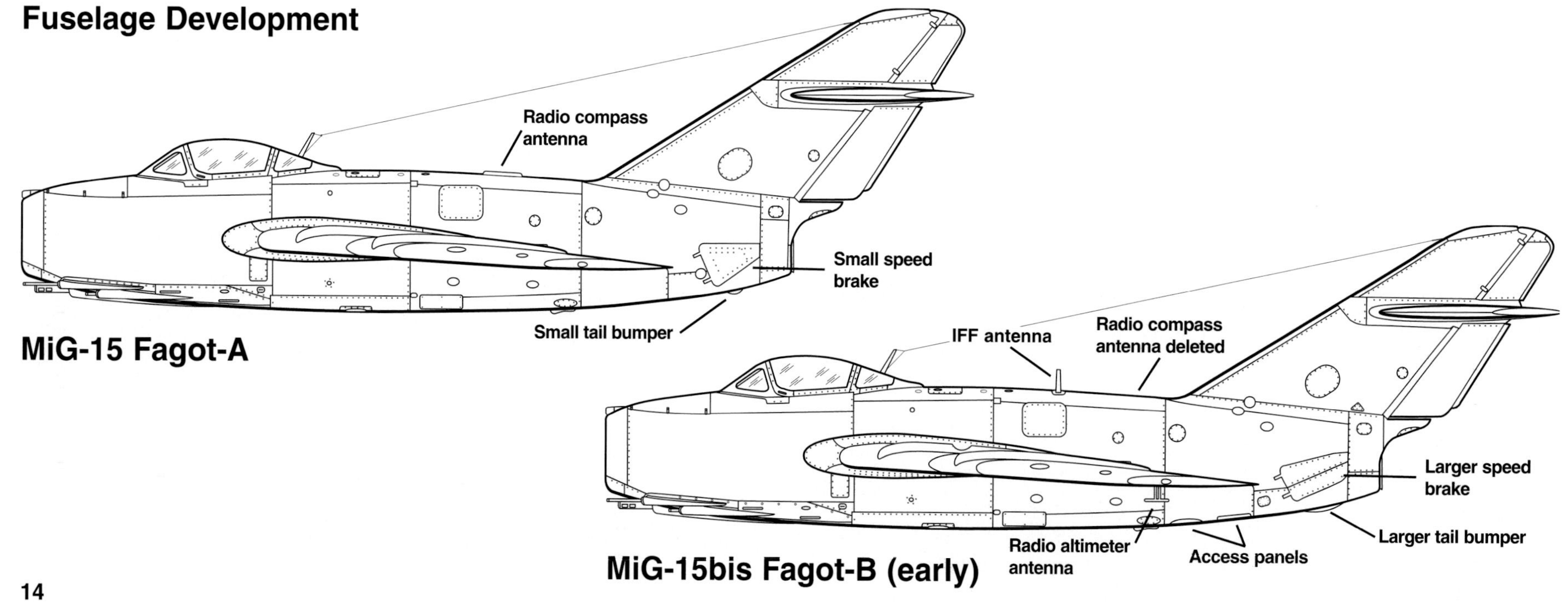

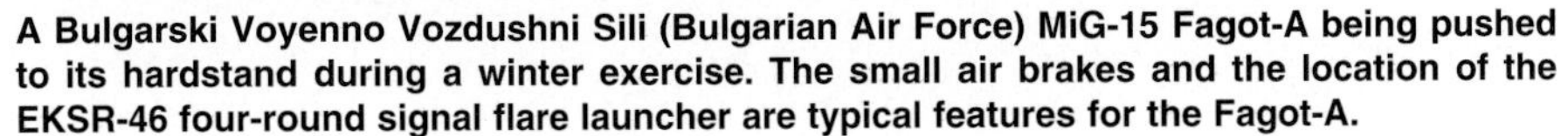

A Bulgarski Voyenno Vozdushni Sili (Bulgarian Air Force) MiG-15 Fagot-A being pushed to its hardstand during a winter exercise. The small air brakes and the location of the EKSR-46 four-round signal flare launcher are typical features for the Fagot-A.

'Red 501,' a freshly completed Lim-2 Fagot-B (serial number 1B-005-01) at the ramp of the PZL (Panstwowe Zaklady Lotnicze — State Aircraft Factory) at Mielec, Poland. This plane carries the early type of antenna but lacks the landing light in the air intake splitter, a feature more typical of late production Fagot-Bs.

A Czechoslovak Air Force S-102 Fagot-A on final approach with the air brakes fully extended. A feature of the MiG-15 was the lack of the rectangular fairing for the MRP-48 marker receiver on the lower rear fuselage.

'Red 2404,' an early production MiG-15bis of the Romanian Air Force, is equipped with two PTB-400 400-liter drop tanks and a MiG-17-type nose wheel as usually found on late production batches of the Fagot-B. It carries the Romanian national markings that were introduced in 1985. At that time a number of MiG-15bis were still in active service in second-line duties such as weather reconnaissance.

All MiG-15 Fagot-As and the early production MiG-15bis Fagot-Bs were equipped with an FS-155 landing light located in the upper portion of the air intake splitter. The S-13 gun camera mounted on the upper lip of the air intake is slightly offset to starboard. Visible is the asymmetric arrangement of the single N-37 cannon on the starboard side and the two NS-23 KM cannons on port. This particular Czechoslovak Air Force MiG-15bis has the standard nose wheel with a long strut.

The majority of the MiG-15bis had the FS-155 landing light relocated to the port wing root and a small, diamond-shaped inlet introduced in the air intake splitter. Most Fagot-Bs were equipped with a large gun blast panel, as on this particular example, a former Hungarian Air Force MiG-15bis equipped with the late type of nose wheel that became standard on the MiG-17 Fresco.

The nose compartment of a former Czechoslovak Air Force MiG-15 Fagot-A. The RSI-6 radio equipment as well as the SRO-1 Bariy-M IFF system were housed in this compartment.

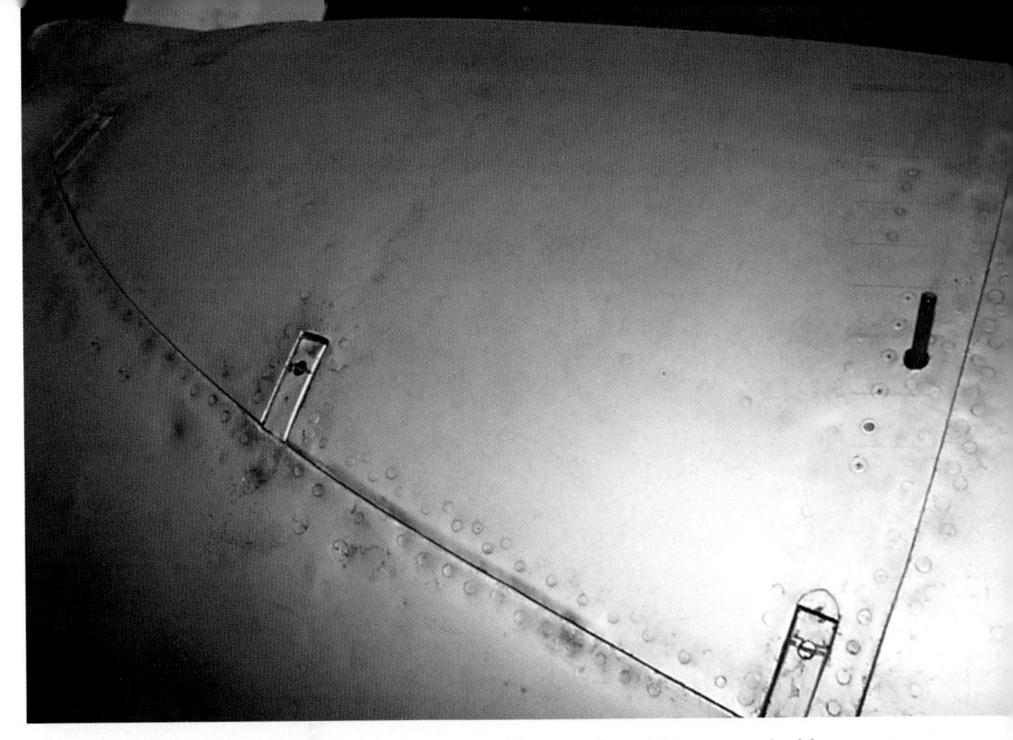

The cover of the radio equipment compartment. The panel could be opened with a snap-lock mechanism. The red rod is the nose wheel position indicator.

The mechanical position indicator for the nose wheel. It was fully retracted when the nose wheel was also retracted but extended as shown here when the MiG-15 was on the ground. There were all-red as well as red-and-white position indicators. The position of the landing gear was also indicated by warning lamps on the instrument panel.

The S-13 gun camera was mounted on top of the air intake. The film capacity was 150 pictures at a speed of eight frames per second. The S-13 and its housing remained identical through the production life of the MiG-15 Fagot.

Maintenance on the RSIU-3 Klyon two-way VHF radio on 'Red 1020,' a Polish-built Lim-2 Fagot-B (serial number 1B-010-20). The air intake is covered and the nozzles of the N-37 and NR-23 cannons sealed by fabric coverings.

The 12A-30 accumulator for the RSIU-3 Klyon radio was charged by an external power supply. For this maintenance work, the nose cover panel was removed. This MiG-15bis, 'Red 144,' belongs to the Bulgarski Voyenno Vozdushni Sili (Bulgarian Air Force).

Ground personnel check 'Red 9,' a late production MiG-15bis (serial number 627766) of the East German Air Force. This particular aircraft was manufactured by the Aero plant at Vodochody in the Czechoslovak Socialist Republic. This late MiG-15bis is unusual in that the diamond-shaped aperture in the upper part of the air intake splitter is missing. Both circular openings in the lower part of the air intake splitter are faired over, a feature often seen on late production MiG-15bis.

The inside of the removable upper nose panel that covered the compartment for the radio and the IFF equipment. The last six digits of the aircraft serial number have been painted inside the panel.

The RSI-6K two-way VHF radio that occupied the nose compartment of an early production MiG-15bis. Part of the covering has been removed from the radio.

The cover of the starboard N-37 37 mm cannon on this early production Hungarian Air Force MiG-15bis Fagot-B has been lowered. The T-shaped RV-2 antenna mounted on the lower part of the nose is a typical feature of early production MiG-15bis. On the majority of Fagot-Bs the antenna was relocated to the lower port wing leading edge.

The port panel for the two NS-23 KM cannons has been lowered. Strengthening ribs are attached to the inner surface of the panel. The rectangular slots are the shell ejection ports. On the NS-23 KM-equipped MiG-15s, these slots were longer and more narrow than on the NR-23-equipped Fagot-B.

The starboard side N-37 cannon of the MiG-15bis was covered by a large fairing. The N-37 weighed 103 kilograms (227 pounds), was recharged by recoil action, and had a rate of fire of 400 rounds per minute. The ammunition supply for the N-37 was 40 rounds.

The starboard shell ejection port on a MiG-15 Fagot-A. The ejection port for the N-37 37 mm cannon were identical on the MiG-15 and MiG-15bis. The 23 mm cannons and the single 37 mm canon were all belt-fed. Belt links and ammunition cases were discarded during firing.

The rear fairing of the N-37 cannon with the blistered shell ejection port placed outside the fairing. On late production MiG-15bis a circular access panel was introduced slightly above the rear N-37 cannon fairing, just above the shell ejection port. The MiG-15 Fagot-A and early MiG-15bis Fagot-B, as shown here, lacked this access panel.

The muzzle of an N-37 37 mm cannon mounted on the starboard side of a Romanian Air Force MiG-15 Fagot-A. This particular Fagot-A has an additional, non-standard gun blast panel on the forward portion of the nose wheel door.

All MiG-15 Fagot-As and early production MiG-15bis Fagot-Bs were equipped with two small gun blast panels. This arrangement of gun blast panels was only used on MiG-15s equipped with the NS-23 KM 23 mm cannon, the standard weapon for all MiG-15 Fagot-A and the early MiG-15bis Fagot-B. The two panels are of different size.

The majority of MiG-15bis Fagot-Bs were equipped with a large, one-piece gun blast panel installed with the new NR-23 23 mm cannon, which replaced the earlier NS-23 KM weapon.

The starboard side part of the gun blast panel for the N-37 37 mm cannon is different in size and shape from the panel on the starboard side. The corner of the panel on the starboard side is behind the panel line.

The port gun blast panel of a MiG-15bis. The port gun blast panel for the NR-23 cannon was slightly different in size and shape from the panel for the NS-23 KM on earlier MiG-15s. The corner of the port blast panel lies exactly on the nose intake panel line.

A Bulgarian pilot climbs into his MiG-15 Fagot-A. The flying gear is typical of Warsaw Pact pilots in the 1950s. The two-piece gun blast panel for the NS-23 KM cannon is clearly visible. For unknown reasons, the starboard aperture in the air intake splitter is open, while that on the port side has been closed.

The nose of 'Red 757,' a Romanian Air Force MiG-15 Fagot-A. The fairings for the NS-23 KM cannon on all MiG-15 Fagot-As and early MiG-15bis Fagot-Bs were much longer than those on the MiG-15bis equipped with the NR-23 cannons. Initially, no gun blast panel was applied to the nose wheel doors. This modification was done during an overhaul.

The two gun blast panels of the MiG-15 Fagot-As and the early MiG-15bis Fagot-Bs equipped with the early NS-23 KM cannon were different in size and asymmetrically applied, as seen on this Fagot-A. The small panel mounted on the centerline lower air intake lip covers the nose jacking point and is attached to the fuselage with two bolts.

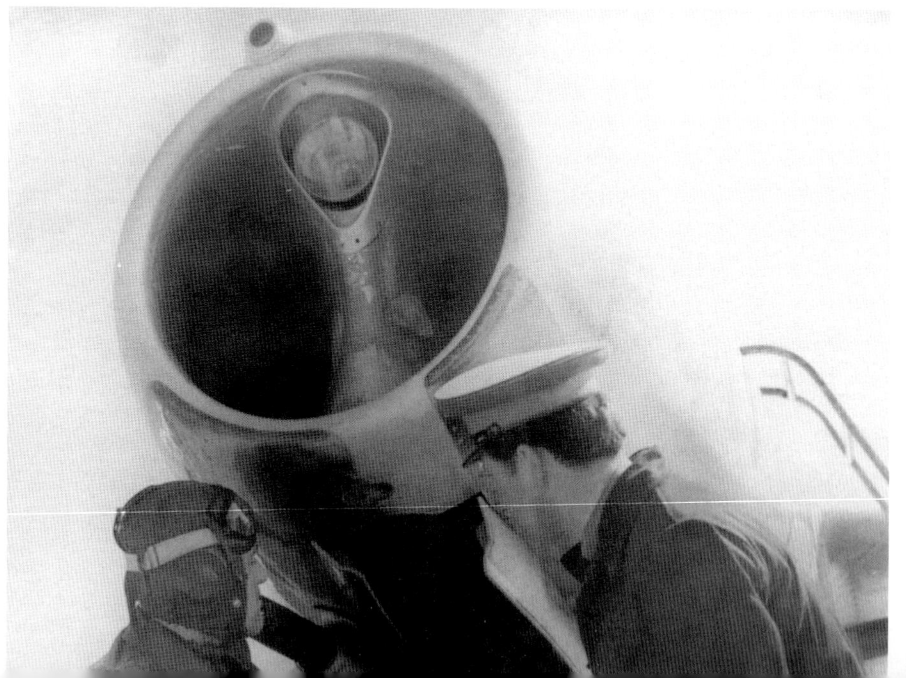

This Romanian Air Force MiG-15 Fagot-A, 'Red 2404,' is unusual in having the starboard side RV-2 radio altimeter antenna applied on the lower fuselage, just above the blistered shell ejection port of the N-37 cannon. Only a few retrofitted MiG-15 Fagot-As and standard production MiG-15bis Fagot-B carried this configuration of the RV-2 antenna. MiG-15 Fagot-As coming off the production line all lacked the RV-2 antenna, while the majority of the MiG-15bis Fagot-Bs had the RV-2 antenna located on the lower port wing tip. A circular access hatch has been retrofitted next to the shell ejection port.

Armament Development

MiG-15bis (early)

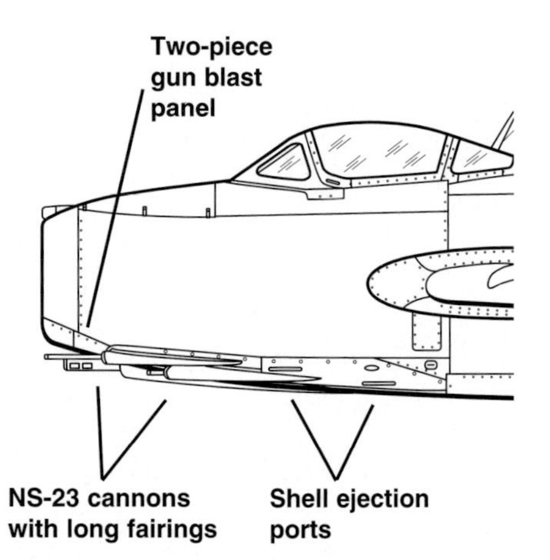

MiG-15bis (late)

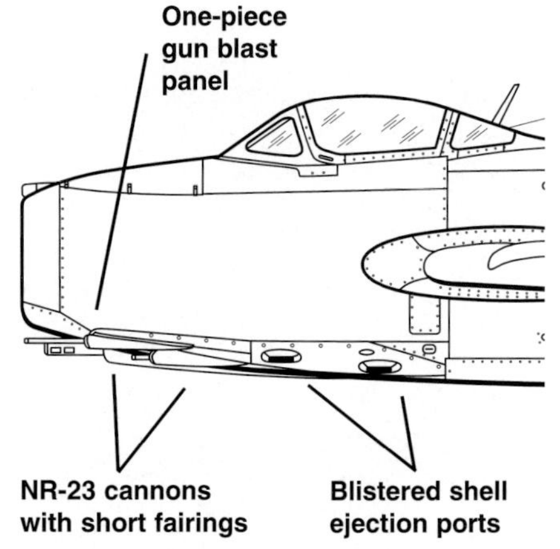

'Red 722,' a late production MiG-15bis (serial number 31530722) of the Hungarian Air Force, displays the short fairings for the cannons as well the blistered shell ejection ports which were typical features of a Fagot-B equipped with the NR-23 cannon. Unusual for this aircraft is that the rectangular aperture in the left blistered shell ejection port is offset to inboard. On standard production MiG-15bis it was located in the centerline of the blister. The size of the port gun blast panel clearly identifies this fighter as a MiG-15bis. This particular Fagot-B was built in late 1952 at Gosudarstvenny Aviatsionny Zavod 31 (State Aircraft Factory 31) at Tbilisi in the Georgian Soviet Socialist Republic and was delivered to the 62. Vadaszrepülö Ezred (62th Fighter Wing) of the Hungarian Air Force on 20 January 1953.

The long fairings of the NS-23 KM cannons on a MiG-15 Fagot-A of the Polish Air Force. The arrangement of the NS-23 KM cannon was identical on the MiG-15 Fagot-A and the early MiG-15bis Fagot-B. Non-standard for Fagot-As is the large gun blast panel retrofitted to the nose wheel door of this aircraft.

The two rectangular shell ejection ports of the NS-23 KM cannon-equipped MiG-15 Fagot-A and MiG-15bis Fagot-B. The long, narrow slots are a typical feature for the NS-23 KM-equipped versions of the Fagot.

The short fairings of the NR-23 23 mm cannon. The NR-23 weapon was installed only on the MiG-15bis, never on the Fagot-A. This particular MiG-15bis of the Polish Air Force is equipped with the late production MiG-17 type nose wheel as retrofitted to many early production MiG-15bis and some MiG-15 Fagot-As.

The blistered shell ejection ports were only installed on the NR-23 cannon equipped MiG-15bis Fagot-B. The slots were shorter but broader than those on the Fagots that were equipped with the early NS-23 KM cannon.

The Polish Air Force relocated the SRO-1 Bariy-M IFF blade antenna from the rear fuselage spine to a location behind the port nose wheel well, offset to port and slightly below the lower fairing for the NR-23 cannon. This position of the antenna is very rarely seen on the Fagot and was only introduced on Polish Air Force MiG-15s late in their operational lives.

The centerline mounted ejection port. In the background is the fairing for the N-37 cannon.

A rarely seen field modification for the MiG-15 and early MiG-15bis equipped with the NS-23 KM cannon was an additional, third, centerline-mounted gun blast panel. The small rectangular panel on the centerline is the jack attachment point. This panel appeared on all MiG-15s.

The lower rear ejection port of the port NR-23 cannon. The NR-23 cannon had an ammunition supply of 80 rounds, which could spent in a single burst of 5.3 seconds.

Forward Fuselage Construction

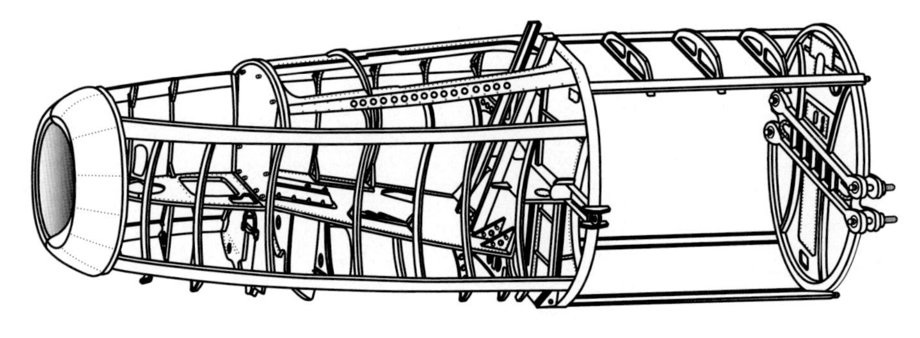

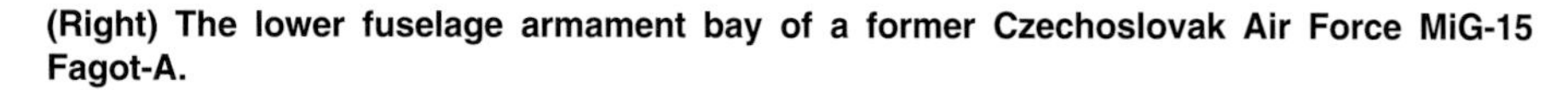

(Right) The lower fuselage armament bay of a former Czechoslovak Air Force MiG-15 Fagot-A.

The port NS-23 KM cannon of a Romanian Air Force MiG-15 Fagot-A. Compared with the NR-23 installation, the front portions of the fairings are different as well as the riveting of the gun blast panel on the lower nose. The small gun blast panels attached to the nose wheel doors are not standard for the Fagot-A and were retrofitted to this aircraft.

The NR-23 cannon armament of a Hungarian Air Force MiG-15bis. A large gun blast panel has been applied on the nose wheel door. The small port gun blast fairing clearly denotes this fighter as a MiG-15bis. The ammunition supply was 80 rounds per cannon.

The armament package of a MiG-15. For servicing, the entire package was lowered by cables attached to the front and rear of the platform. Lifting of the platform was performed by a built-in winch.

The armament package of a MiG-15 on its servicing trolley. Maintenance and re-arming was accomplished much more easily on the MiG-15 than on the contemporary North American F-86 Sabre.

The armament platform of a late production MiG-15bis of the Bulgarian Air Force is lowered for servicing. This Fagot-B has been equipped with the same nose wheel as the MiG-17 Fresco.

A Bulgarian Air Force MiG-15bis being rearmed. The ammunition boxes for the three cannons were mounted on top of the weapons. Initial charging of the 23 mm cannons and the single 37 mm cannon was done pneumatically.

This type of nose wheel was mounted on the majority of MiG-15s. In contrast to the main wheels, the nose wheel was not equipped with a brake. The nose wheel of the MiG-15 is retracted and lowered hydraulically with a pneumatic emergency backup system.

The modified, MiG-17-type nose wheel installed on late production MiG-15bis Fagot-Bs. The castoring nosewheel can turn 50 degrees right or left for taxying. A number of MiG-15 Fagot-As and early MiG-15bis Fagot-Bs were retrofitted with the late-type nose wheel.

The standard nose wheel of the MiG-15 Fagot-A and the majority of MiG-15bis Fagot-Bs. The rim on the nose wheel is typical for the MiG-15.

The standard nose wheel of the MiG-15 Fagot-A.

Front view of the standard nose wheel of Fagot-As and the majority of Fagot-Bs.

The standard nose wheel for the MiG-15 had a longer strut.

The late production nose wheel for the MiG-15bis later became standard on the MiG-17.

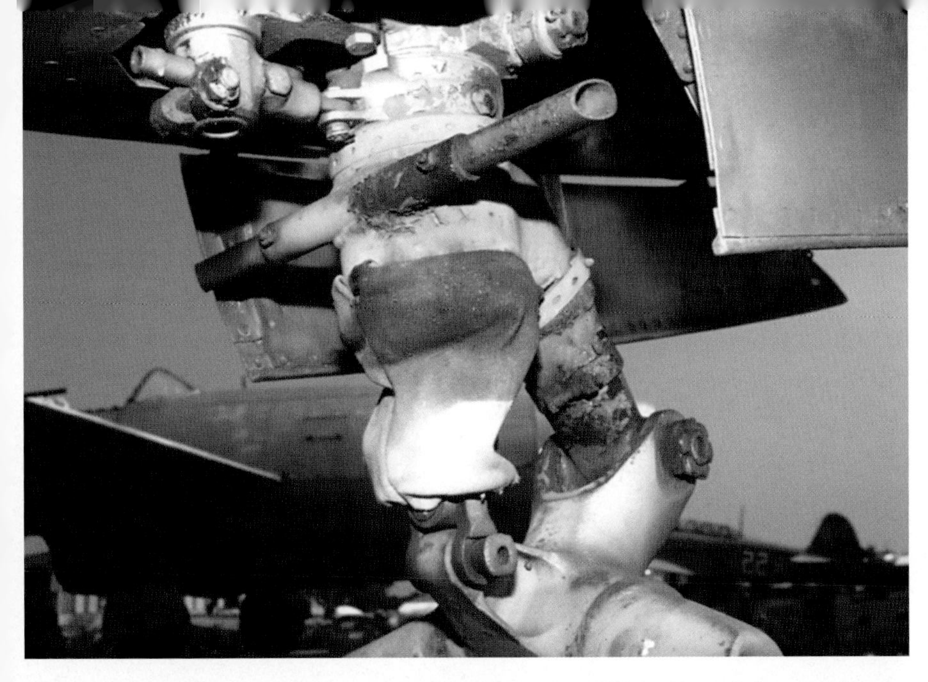

The rear part of the nose gear strut of a late production MiG-15. Part of the strut is covered by a leather sleeve.

Looking up and aft inside the nose wheel well of a late production Fagot-B. The hinges for opening and closing the main wheel doors are clearly visible. The hydraulic cylinder to port (the silver strut seen to right in this photo) retracted the nose gear. The hydraulic system was powered by a pump attached to the engine accessory gearbox and operated at a pressure of 140 bars (4,134 psi). The diamond-shaped green light on the nose wheel strut is rarely seen on MiG-15s.

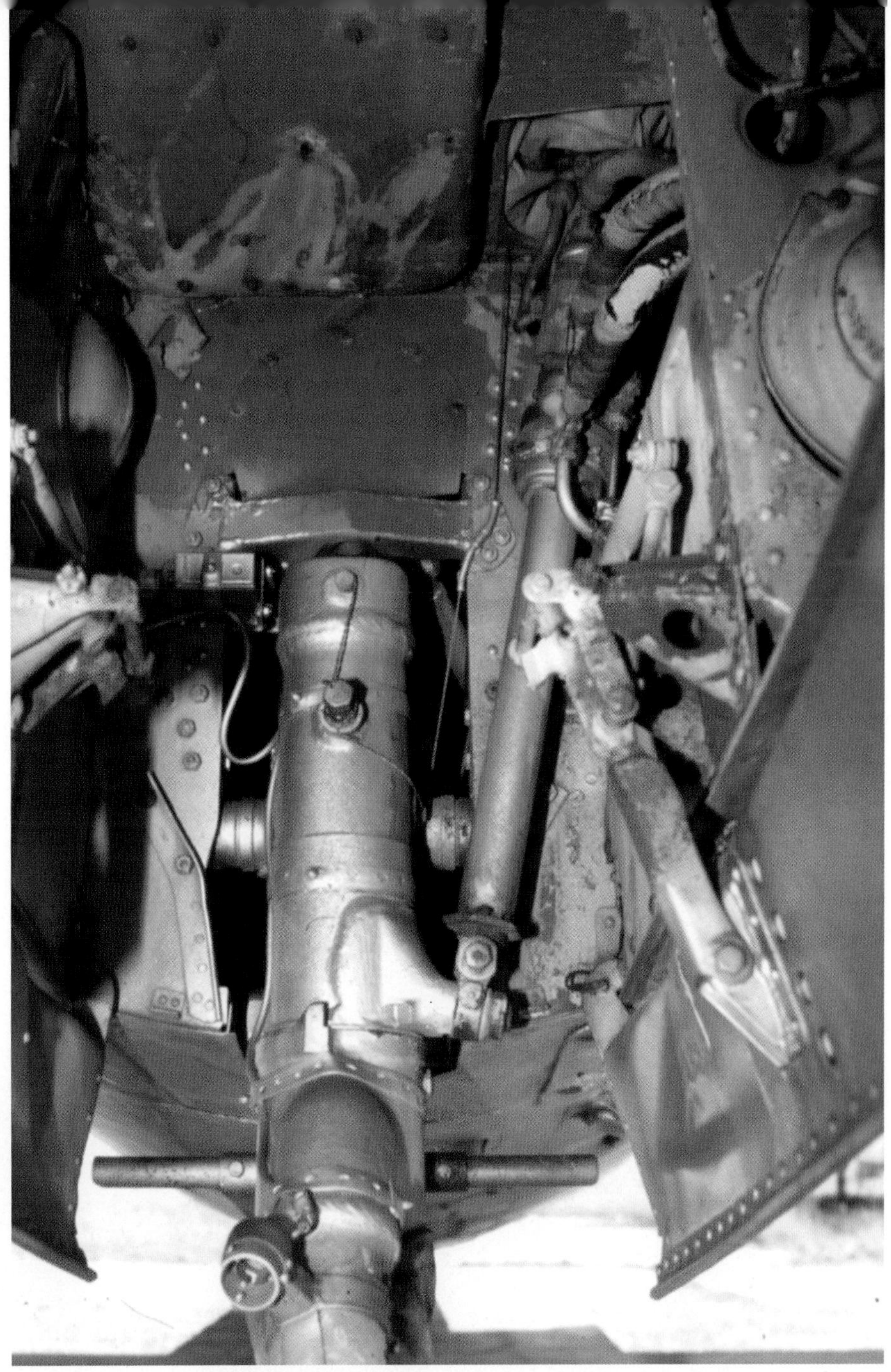

A late production nose wheel well and nose wheel strut. The position light bulb has been removed from its socket. The position light indicated to the waiting ground crew that the nose wheel was properly extended.

A Hungarian ground crew member removes the small panel on the lower air intake lip to expose the nose jacking point. This is an early production MiG-15bis as identified by the FS-155 landing light in the air intake splitter. This particular Fagot-B is equipped with the late production-type nose wheel that later became standard on the MiG-17 Fresco.

Romanian soldiers remove canvas covers from a MiG-15 Fagot-A. The late production nose wheel was retrofitted during an overhaul. The N-37 cannon barrel has received a leather cover.

The small panel, fixed with two bolts, which had to be removed before a a MiG-15 could be jacked up for inspection. This panel was identical on all MiG-15 fighter and trainer versions.

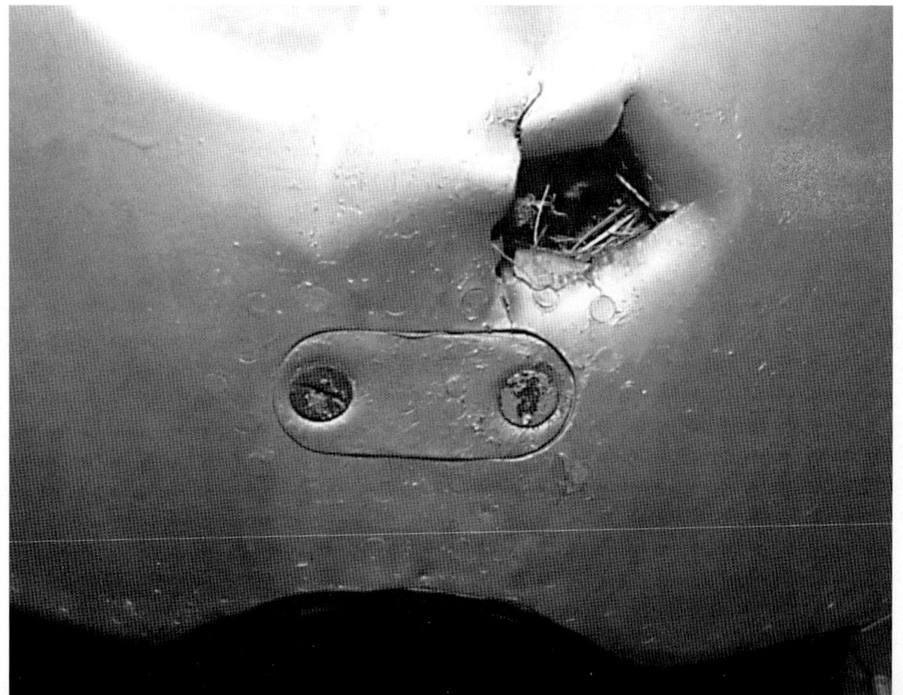

Landing Gear

Nose wheel and strut

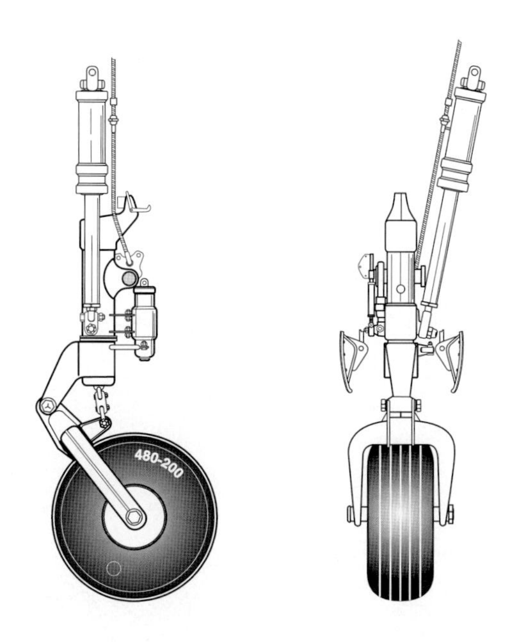

Main wheel and strut

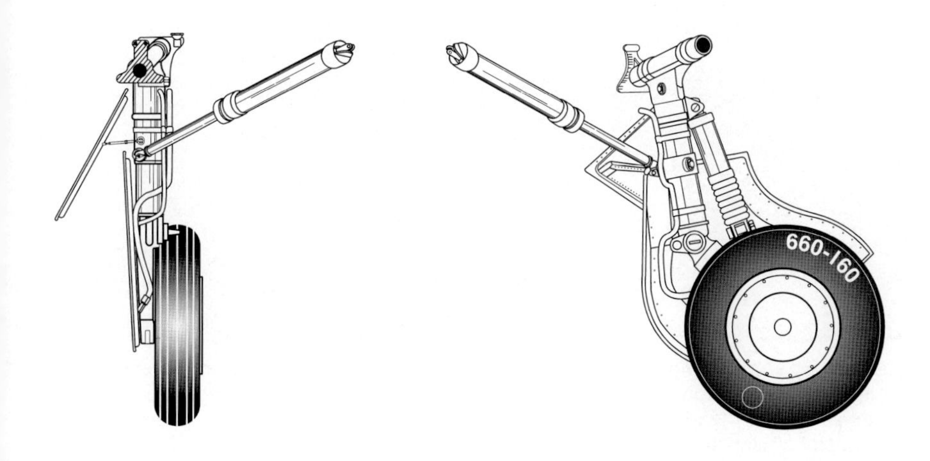

A late production Lim-2 of the Polish Air Force equipped with a nose wheel of the type that later became standard on the MiG-17 Fresco. The size and shape of the port gun blast panel identifies this fighter as a Fagot-B. The diamond-shaped aperture in the upper air intake splitter is another typical feature of the MiG-15.

The port console of a late production Lim-2 Fagot-B and left portion of the instrument panel. The inscriptions on Polish Air Force MiG-15bis were in both Polish and Russian. The red handle is the canopy emergency release, which is located on both sides of the instrument panel.

The port console of a Lim-2 with the POM throttle, painted in yellow. The button in the throttle handle is for radio communication. Below the throttle control is the speed brake lever. The yellow, green, red, and white buttons above and to the left of the throttle are to activate individual flares of the EKSR-46 flare dispenser.

The cockpit of a Czechoslovak-built MiG-15bis Fagot-B with the ASP-3N gunsight mounted atop the instrument panel. On the right is visible the electric panel with its various switches. The white stripe is an aid to spin recovery; in case of a spin, the pilot aligned the control stick with the stripe.

The port console of a MiG-15bis SB, a Czechoslovak derivative of the MiG-15bis Fagot-B. The ARK-5 radio control box has been mounted on the starboard side aft of the console. Inscriptions on the instruments and buttons are in both Czech and Russian.

The control stick with the trigger for firing the guns retracted. This system of firing control was adapted from World War II Luftwaffe fighter aircraft.

The rear part of the port console of a Lim-2. The round black object above the lap strap is the oxygen control.

The starboard side console with the electrical switches located above the emergency undercarriage release (front) and the emergency flap release (rear).

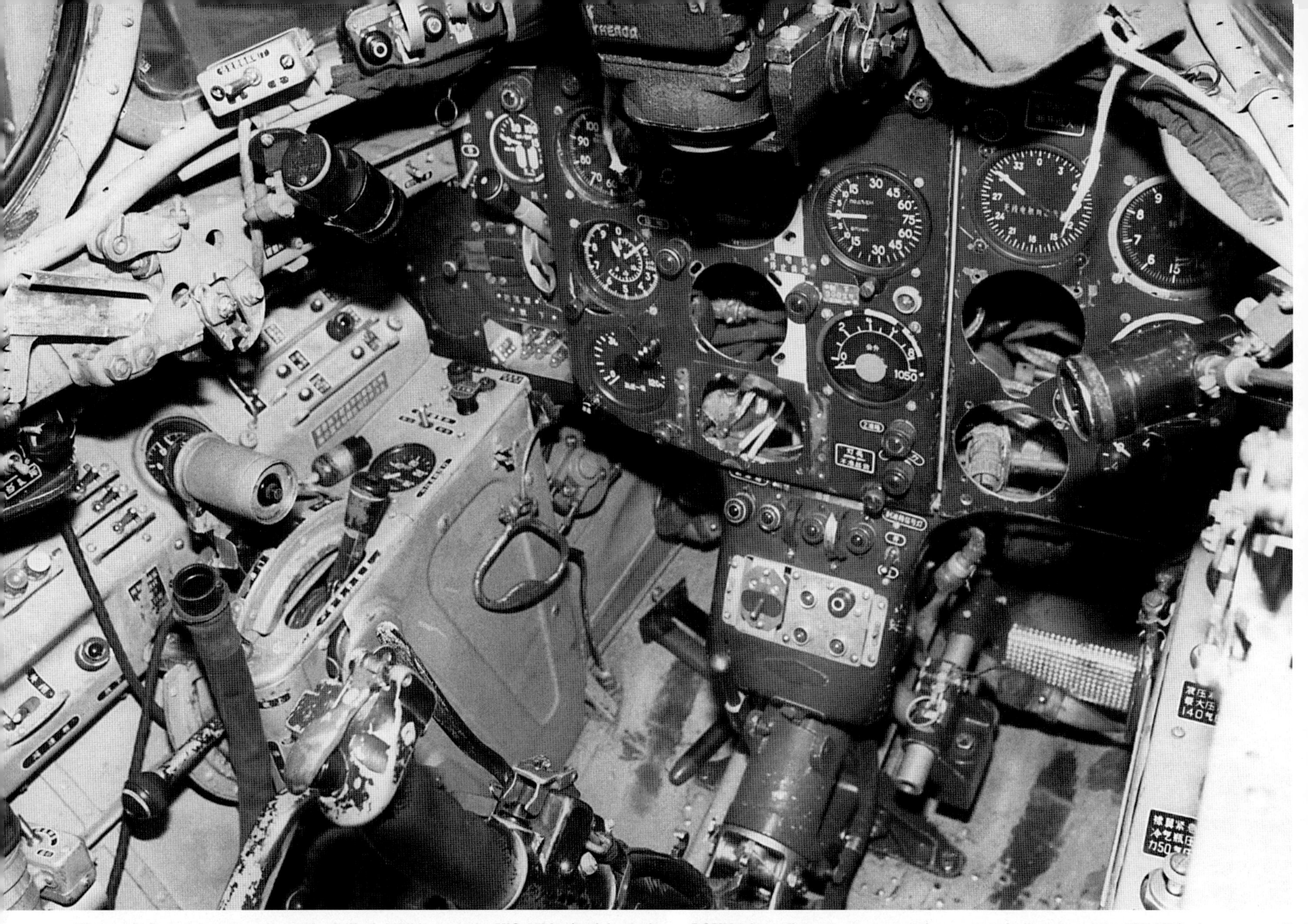

The cockpit and instrument panel of 'Red 2057,' an early MiG-15bis (serial number 2015337) of the North Korean Air Force. Most of the inscriptions are in Korean, but some Cyrillic letters remained. This particular Fagot-B was built by the Gosudarstvenny Aviatsionny Zavod 153 (State Aircraft Factory 153) at Novosibirsk. The EUP-46 turn indicator as well the ACCHO clock are missing from the centerline panel. Also missing are the DGMK-3 long distance gyromagnetic compass indicator and the EMI-3R fuel pressure, oil pressure, and temperature indicator on the starboard side panel. Below the main panel is the external weapon control panel. The cockpit was pressurized by engine bleed air. 'Red 2057' was flown by defecting NKAF pilot Lt. Ro Kim Suk and is now in the U.S. Air Force Museum, Dayton, Ohio.

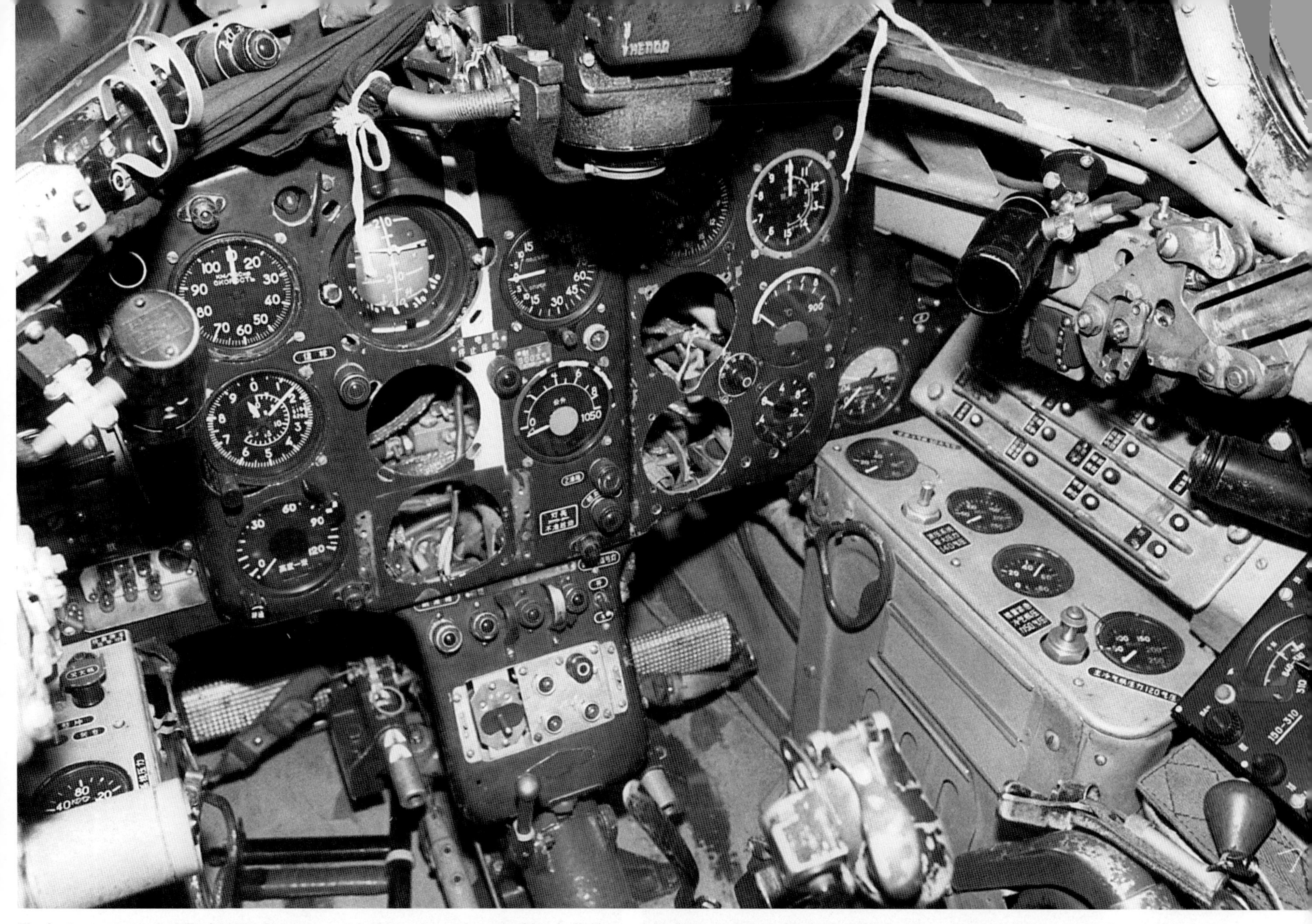

The instrument panel of 'Red 2057.' At top to port is the undercarriage position indicator, below that the DV-17 altimeter, and at bottom the RV-2 radar altimeter indicator. At top immediately to left of the white bar is the AGK-47 artificial horizon; the two instruments below it are missing. The instrument at top on the right side of the white bar is the VAR-75 rate of climb indicator and below it is the KES-857 fuel gauge. The first instrument on top of the starboard side is the ARK-5 radio compass indicator, while the two instruments below it are missing. On the right side of the instrument panel are (top to bottom) the TE-20 engine speed indicator, the TGZ-47 gas temperature gauge, and the EM-10 fuel pressure gauge. On the extreme right is the UVPD-3 cabin pressure altimeter.

The external weapons control panel was attached under the main instrument panel. There were a variety of such control panels manufactured. This particular panel was installed in a Polish-built Lim-2 and differs from the weapons control panel seen in the cockpit of the North Korean MiG-15bis 'Red 2057.'

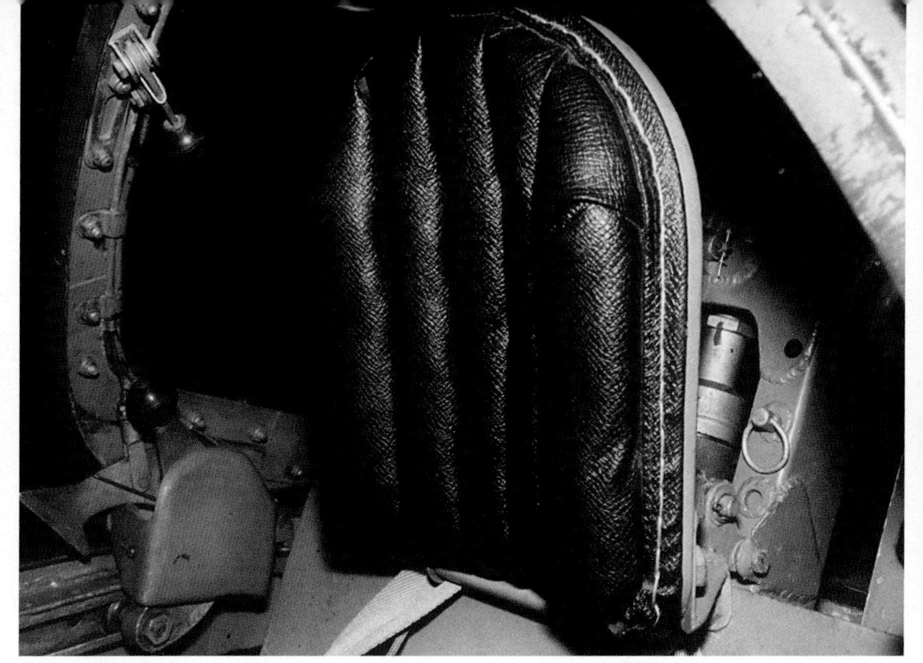

The headrest of the MiG-15bis ejection seat. Behind it can be seen a portion of the ejection seat rails.

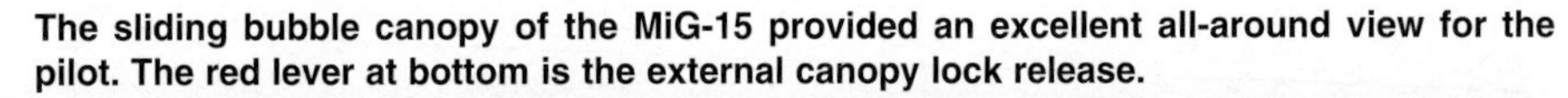

The sliding bubble canopy of the MiG-15 provided an excellent all-around view for the pilot. The red lever at bottom is the external canopy lock release.

The external canopy locking release of a Lim-2 Fagot-B. The canopy could be locked from either the inside or the outside of the cockpit.

The starboard interior canopy locking mechanism. A canopy lock was located on both sides of the cockpit.

With the rear glazing missing the structure of the sliding canopy and its aft window are visible. Most of the canopy glazing on this Hungarian MiG-15bis has been smashed.

The canopy area of a MiG-15bis. The missing rear glazing reveals the cutouts in the frame of the aft portion of the canopy. The antenna mast belongs to the RSI-6K radio. The small device slightly below is the small mast for the wire antenna.

The small mast for the wire antenna was made of wood to guarantee isolation from the alloy airframe of the MiG-15.

Looking down and forward into the cockpit of 'Red 2057' of the North Korean Air Force. The sliding canopy has been removed. A black rubber seal surrounds the pressurized portion of the cockpit.

The rear portion of the headrest and the two rails on which the ejection seat was mounted.

The canopy rail of a Hungarian Air Force MiG-15bis.

The instrument panel of 'Red 2057' with the ASP-3N gyroscopic gun sight.

Ejection Seat

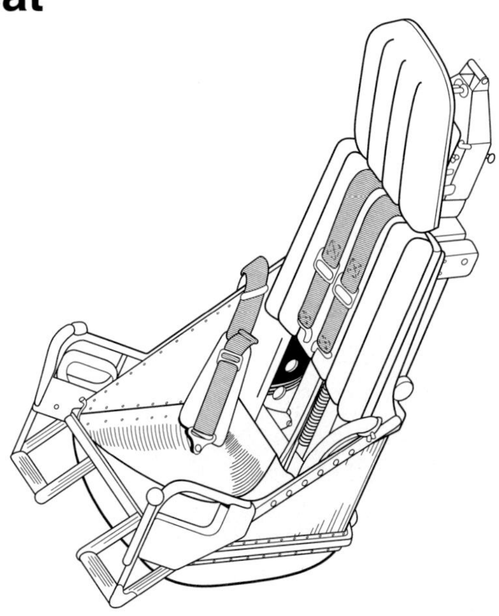

Instrument Panel

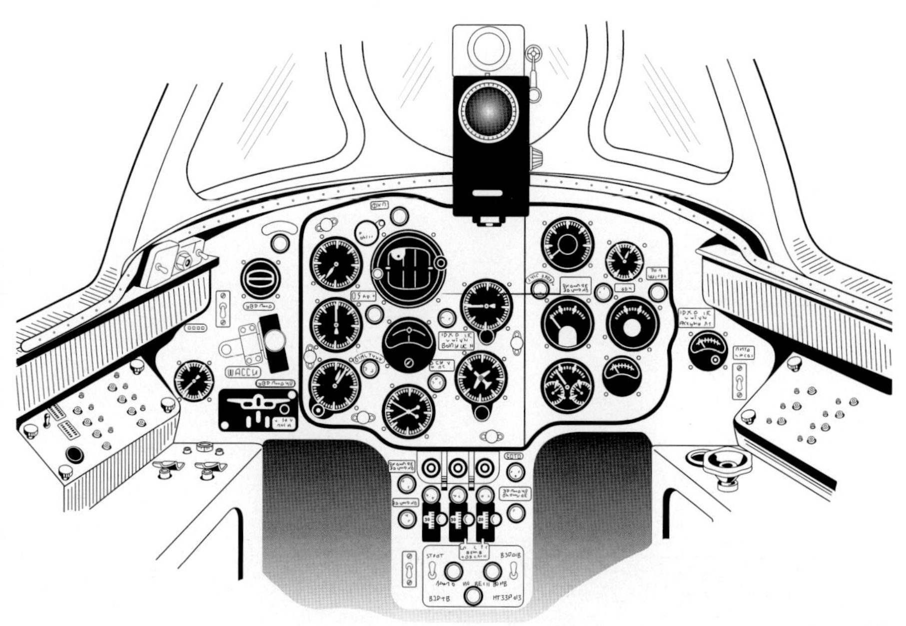

The wing of the MiG-15 and MiG-15bis were externally identical. The starboard aileron had no trim tab. A pitot tube was mounted on the starboard wing. The starboard inner wing fence never had a cutout.

The trim tab on the port aileron of a MiG-15 Fagot-A. This feature remained unchanged throughout the entire production cycle of the MiG-15 and MiG-15bis.

Part of the starboard outboard wing fence with several access panels on the upper surface. The red-white-red landing gear position indicator was placed between the two wing fences. The square panel on the wing leading edge is not standard and is probably the result of a repair.

The hinge of the aileron trim tab was covered with a fairing on the lower surface of the wing.

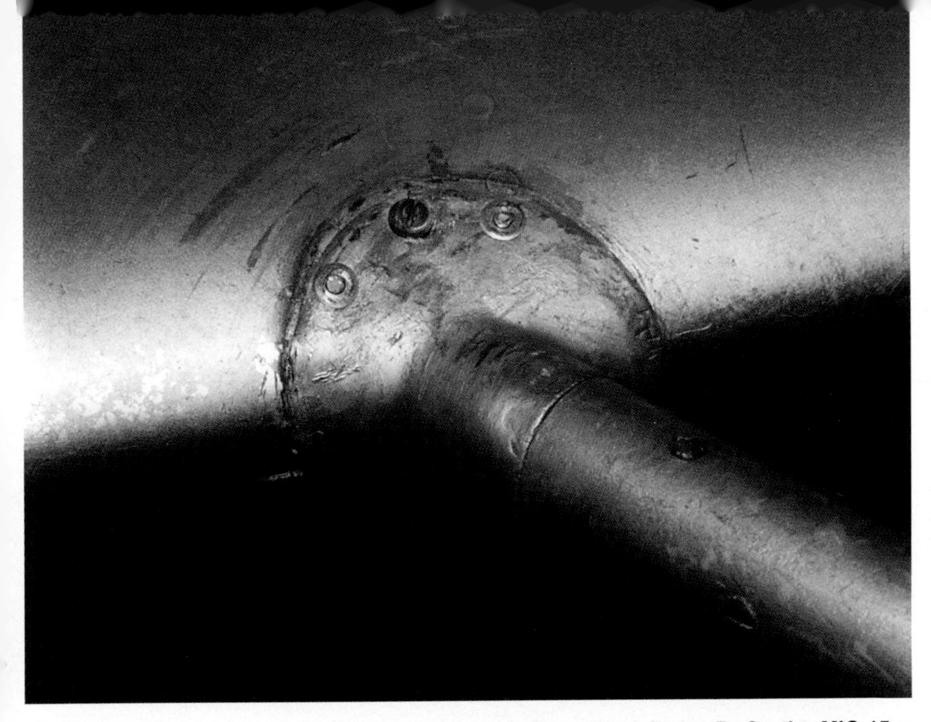

The attachment of the pitot tube on a late production Lim-2 Fagot-B. On the MiG-15 a single pitot tube was mounted in the middle of the starboard wing leading edge.

The pitot tube of a Lim-2 Fagot-B. Throughout the MiG-15's production cycle, the pitot tube remained unchanged.

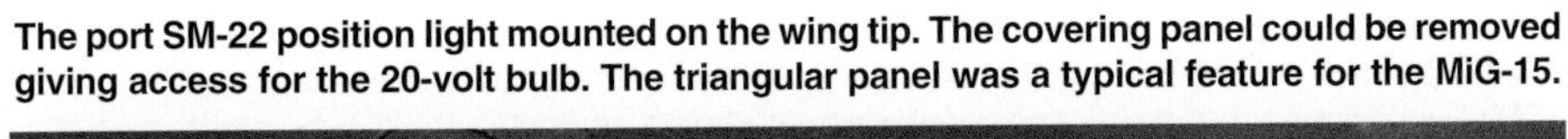

The port SM-22 position light mounted on the wing tip. The covering panel could be removed giving access for the 20-volt bulb. The triangular panel was a typical feature for the MiG-15.

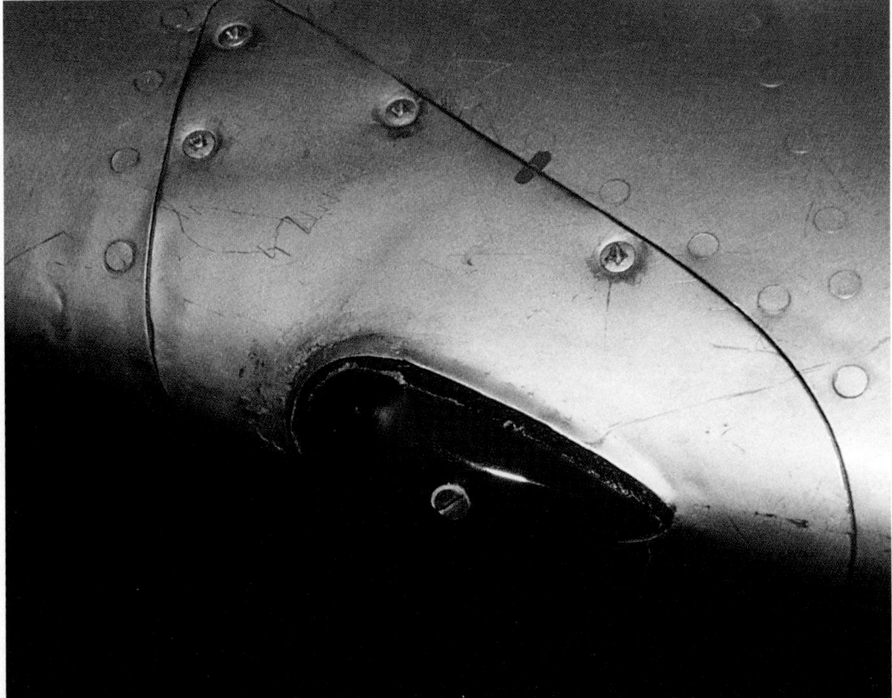

The SM-22 position light on the port wingtip of a Czechoslovak Air Force MiG-15bis Fagot-B. The one-piece wing tip is a typical feature of the MiG-15.

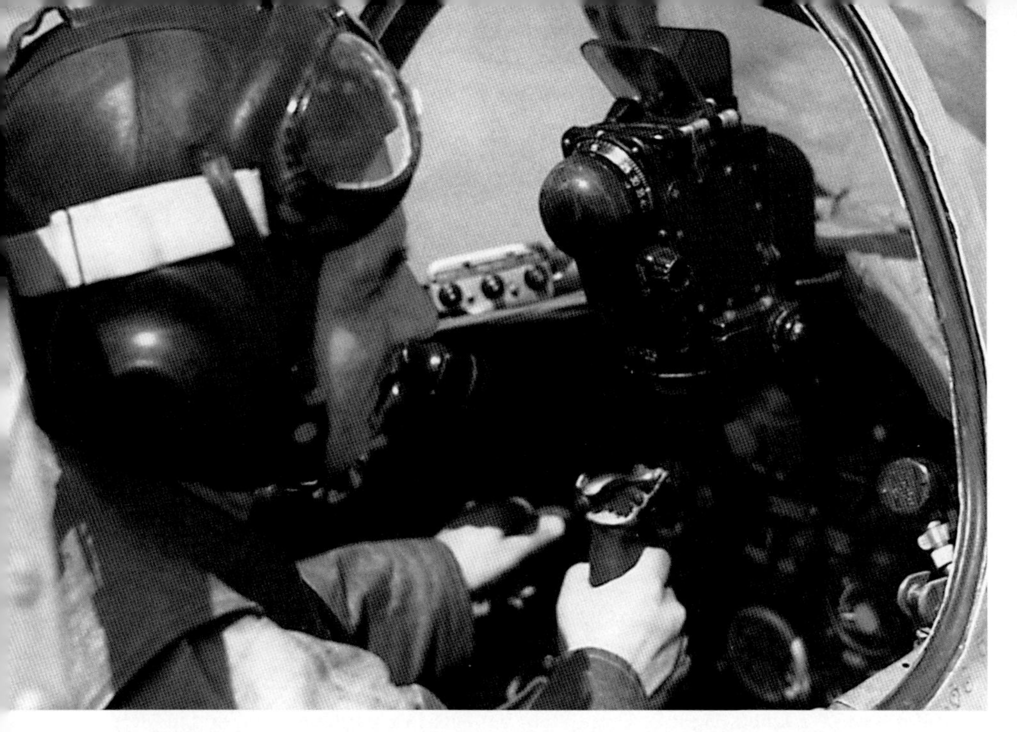

The ASP-1N gun sight obscured a large sector of the MiG-15 pilot's forward view. Leather helmets were typical pilot headgear in the early years of MiG-15 operations.

Throttle Quadrant

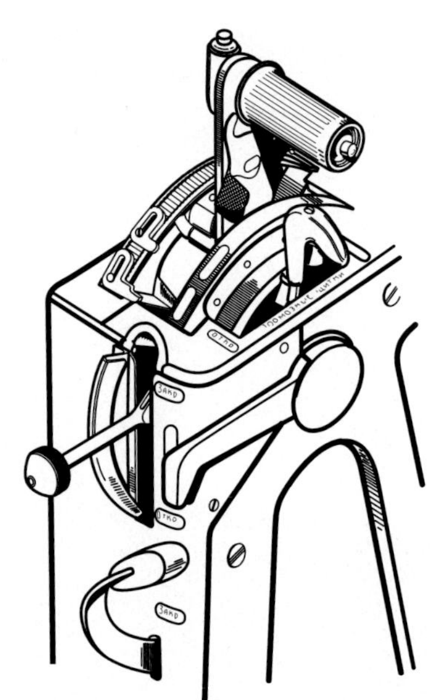

Flight Controls

A ground crewman opens the nose compartment on a Bulgarian Air Force MiG-15bis. The rod visible just above the rear latch is the position indicator for the nose wheel. The MiG-15bis immediately behind is completely covered with canvas.

A Polish pilot climbs into Lim-1 'Red 728' (serial number 1A07028) during an exercise in the mid-1950s. The Lim-1 was the Polish copy of the MiG-15 Fagot-A. The small platform on which the antenna mast rests is non-standard for the Fagot-A but became standard on the late production MiG-15bis Fagot-B.

'Red 820,' a Polish Air Force Lim-2 (serial number 1B00820). The circular access hatch above the shell ejection port (just visible at bottom left) was a field modification done on many Warsaw Pact Fagot-Bs.

Four Hungarian Fagot-B pilots prepare for a mission. Their flying suits are typical for the mid-1950s. The aircraft nearest camera, 'Red 827,' is a MiG-15bis (serial number 31530827) followed by 'Red 906' (serial number 31530906) and 'Red 812' (serial number 31530812). Note the red arrow barely visible on the slipper tank of 'Red 906.'

In the mid-1950s the leather flying suit was replaced by a more advanced fabric suit for the MiG-15 pilots, and the helmet was also improved. This Czechoslovak-built S-102 (serial number 323614) carried the tactical number 'LN-03' in black.

The radar warning antenna was applied under the wing, just in front of the main wheel well. The circular panel is typical feature for the MiG-15; the later MiG-17 had an oval, offset panel.

The wing root fairing has been removed from this Czechoslovak-built MiG-15bis. A typical modification of Czechoslovak Air Force Fagot-Bs was the introduction of a reinforcing strip, which wrapped around the leading edge, on the upper portion of the wing root fairing. The wing root fairing on Soviet-built MiG-15s was more pointed than on Czechoslovak-built Fagot-Bs.

This Soviet-built MiG-15bis lacks the the wing root fairing reinforcing strip introduced on Czechoslovak-built Fagot-Bs. The front part of the fairing is more pointed than on the Czech built MiG-15bis. The riveting on the fairing is not aligned, a sign of the poor craftsmanship seen on Soviet-built Fagot-Bs.

This Czechoslovak-built MiG-15bis is equipped with an additional reinforcing strip above the wing root fairing. This is an unique feature of Czech Air Force MiG-15s. Some of the access hatches on the fuselages of Czechoslovak-built MiG-15s were circular and not oval as on Soviet-built Fagots.

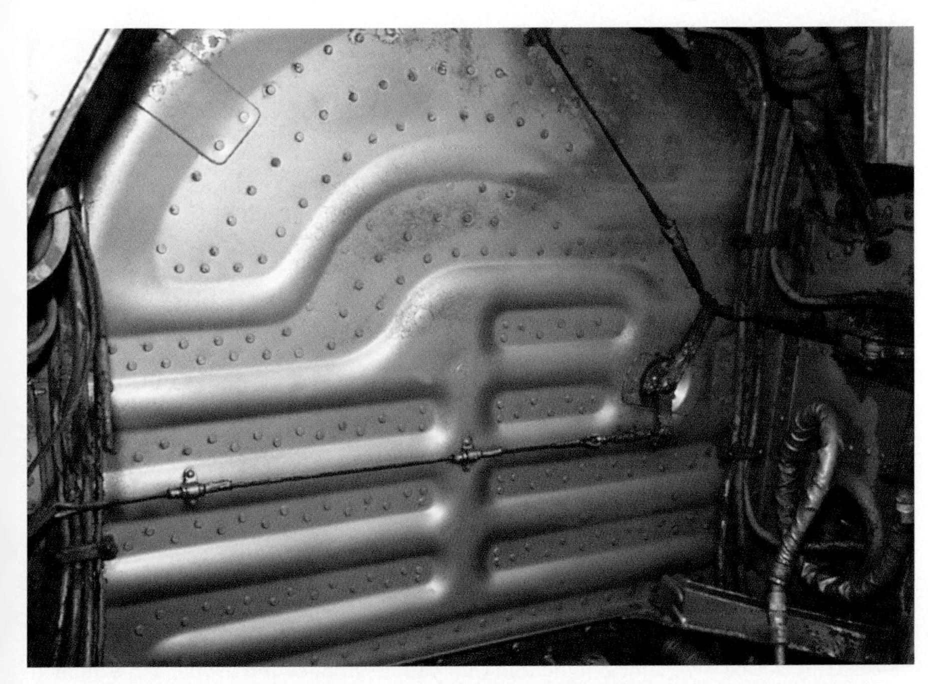

The port main gear well contains a number of pneumatic tubes and electrical wires.

The rear part of the starboard main gear well. Note the pulley for the main gear and main gear cover plate mechanism.

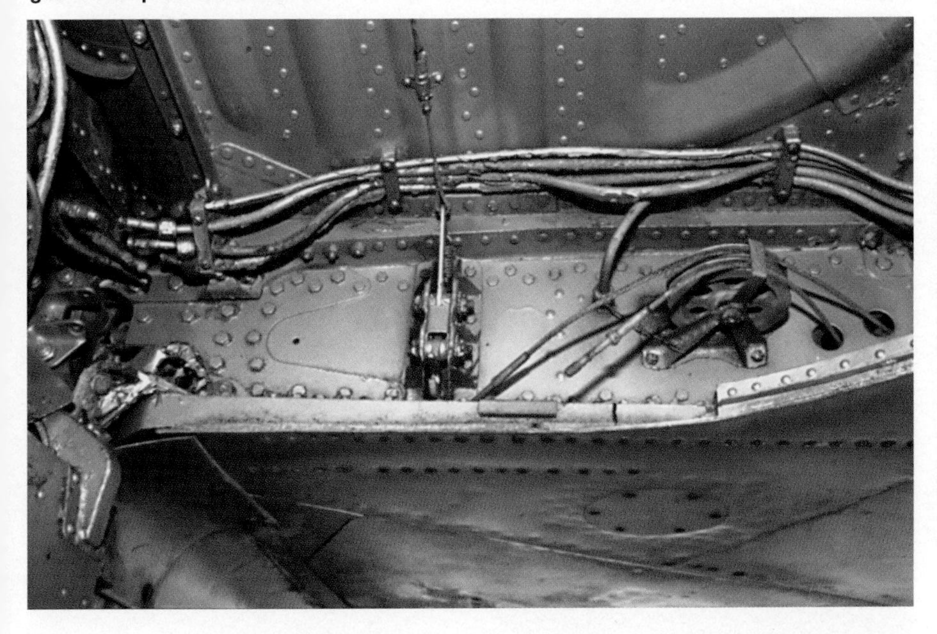

The starboard wing root and wheel well of a MiG-15bis. The wooden transport cradle was typical for the transportation of MiG-15s by road or train.

Wing Flaps

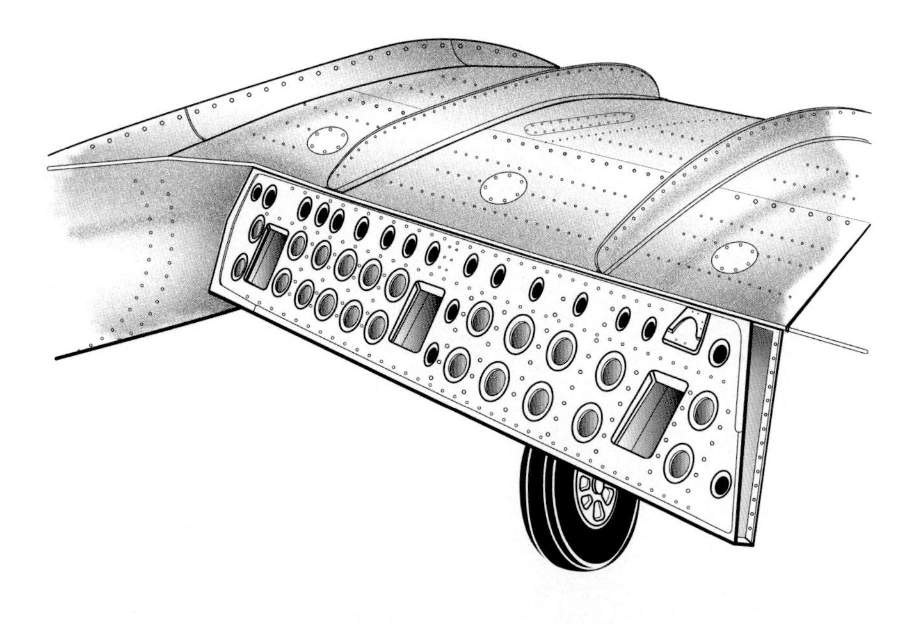

The wing flaps could be lowered independently. The circular apertures cut in the upper surface of the flap reduced weight.

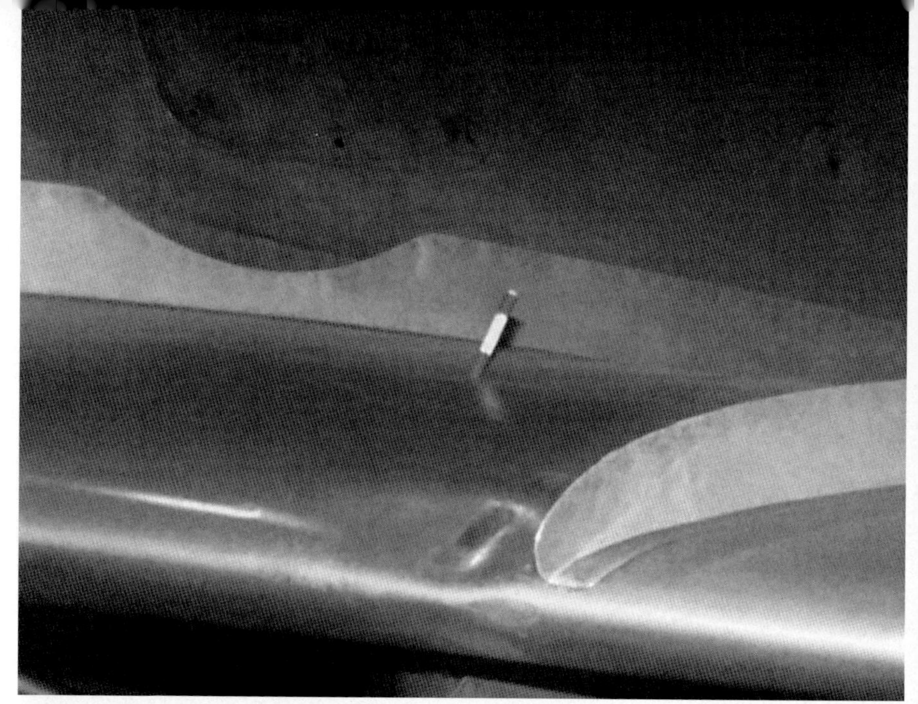

The mechanical position indicator for the main gear was located between the two wing fences. This device was painted either red with a white stripe or red overall and extended above the wing surface when the landing gear was lowered.

The fully extended starboard Fowler-type flap of a MiG-15 reveals details of the wing construction. One of the three rails on which the flap was mounted can be seen at lower right.

Polish MiG-15bis were modified with a Sirena 2 radar homing and warning system. One of the button-shaped antennas for the system was placed on the wing leading edge. This Lim-2 is equipped with PTB-400 400-liter drop tanks.

The button-shaped antenna of the Sirena 2 radar homing and warning system that was retrofitted to the rear of the wingtip. No MiG-15bis was ever built with this device as standard.

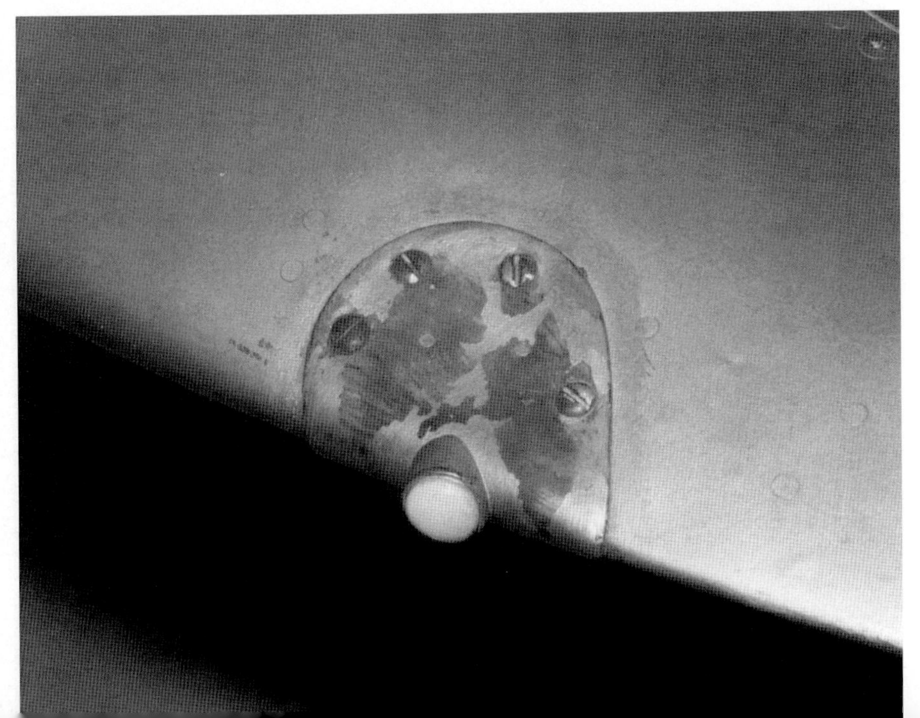

The Sirena 2 antennas were located on the rear wing tip behind the position light as well on the outer wing leading edge, as seen on this two-seat MiG-15 UTI.

PTB-260 260-liter slipper tanks were initially mounted on all MiG-15bis. This device was subsequently replaced by the PTB-400 drop tank.

The nose portion of the PTB-260 slipper tank on a MiG-15 Fagot-A. There was just one refueling point on the PTB-260.

The PTB-400 drop tanks were provided with two refueling caps. The front refueling point was placed in front of the hard point.

The tail of the PTB-400 drop tank on a MiG-15bis. A second refueling point with cap was located on the aft portion of the tank.

This Romanian Air Force MiG-15 was equipped with a ventilation device on top of the PTB-400 drop tank. Not all MiG-15s were so equipped.

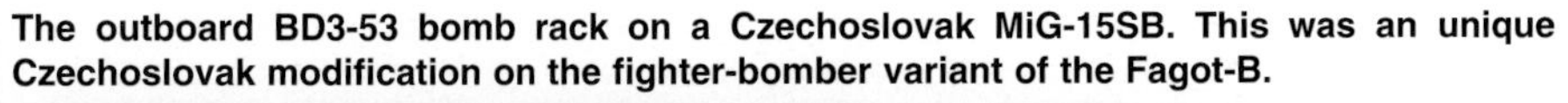

The outboard BD3-53 bomb rack on a Czechoslovak MiG-15SB. This was an unique Czechoslovak modification on the fighter-bomber variant of the Fagot-B.

The inboard BD3-53 bomb rack equipped with a launching rail for the LR-130 unguided missile, a weapon that was developed by the Czechoslovakian Air Force.

Attachment point for the BD3-53 bomb rack on the port wing. This hard point also accomodated the PTB-400 drop tank.

Wing Fences

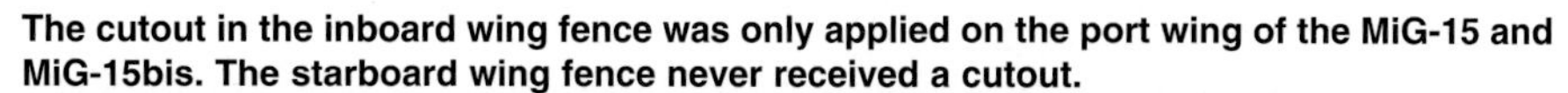
The cutout in the inboard wing fence was only applied on the port wing of the MiG-15 and MiG-15bis. The starboard wing fence never received a cutout.

Most MiG-15s had a ‘cutout’ in the port inner wing fence to enable the pilot to better see the flap position indicator. This feature was not related to any specific version, as wing fences with and without the cutout were found on Fagot-As as well as Fagot-Bs.

This Hungarian Air Force MiG-15 Fagot-A is equipped with an inboard wing fence without a cutout. Wing fences without cutouts were found on some Soviet and Czechoslovak-built MiG-15s. Polish-manufactured Fagots all had a cutout in the port inner wing fence.

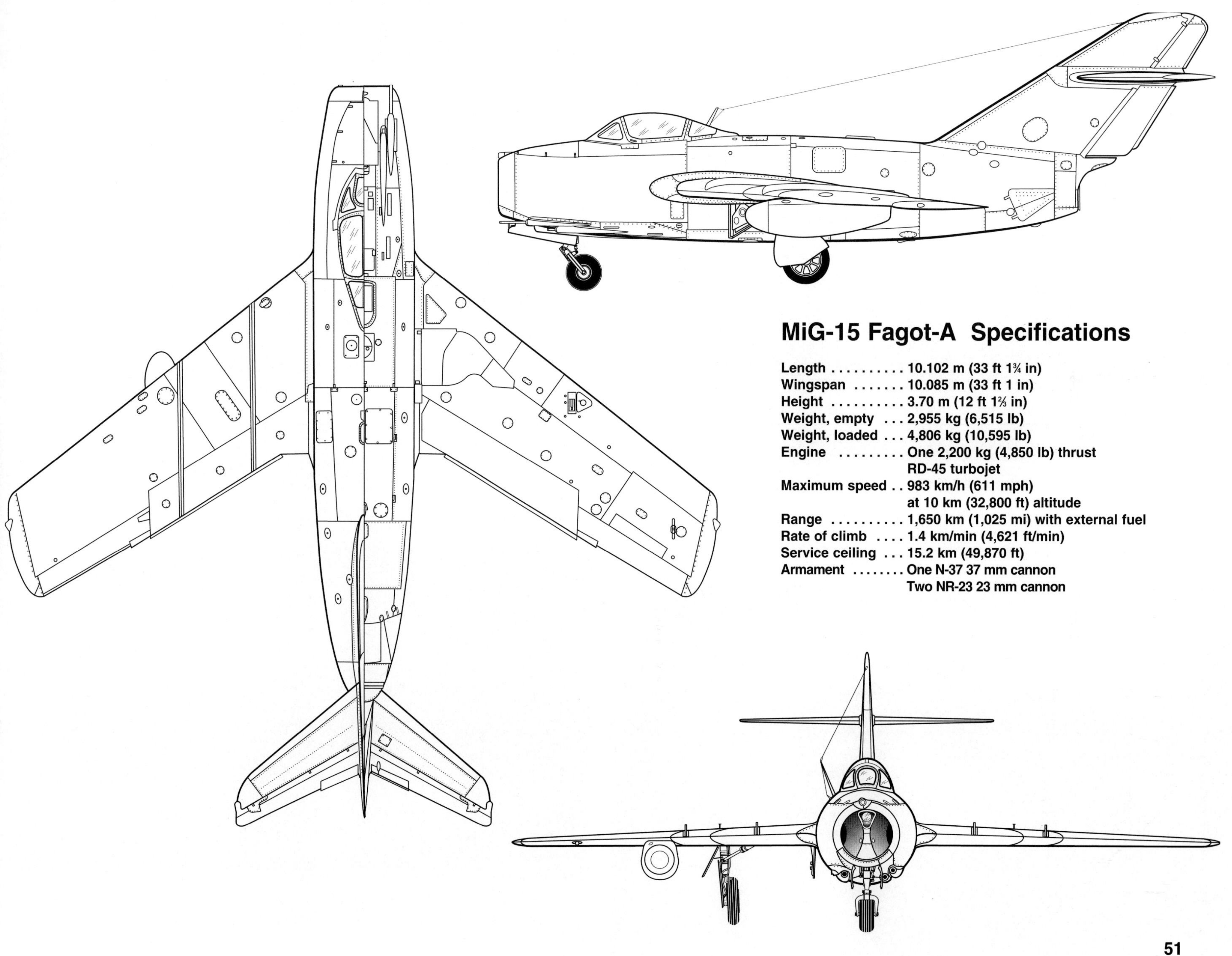

MiG-15 Fagot-A Specifications

Length	10.102 m (33 ft 1¾ in)
Wingspan	10.085 m (33 ft 1 in)
Height	3.70 m (12 ft 1⅔ in)
Weight, empty	2,955 kg (6,515 lb)
Weight, loaded	4,806 kg (10,595 lb)
Engine	One 2,200 kg (4,850 lb) thrust RD-45 turbojet
Maximum speed	983 km/h (611 mph) at 10 km (32,800 ft) altitude
Range	1,650 km (1,025 mi) with external fuel
Rate of climb	1.4 km/min (4,621 ft/min)
Service ceiling	15.2 km (49,870 ft)
Armament	One N-37 37 mm cannon Two NR-23 23 mm cannon

The starboard inboard main wheel hub of a MiG-15.

The outboard main wheel on a MiG-15bis. The large circular aperture in front of the main wheel well is the retractable LFSV-45 landing light, which had been removed from this particular Hungarian Fagot and covered by a circular alloy panel. Inner and outer rims of the main wheel were different.

The port main landing gear of a MiG-15 Fagot-A. The main wheels remained identical throughout the production cycle of this Soviet fighter. The single hydraulic line is a typical feature of the MiG-15.

The two cover doors for the port main landing gear on a Czechoslovak Air Force MiG-15SB Fagot-B. All MiG-15 versions used identical main gear cover doors.

The main gear doors of a Czechoslovak-built MiG-15SB. The flush covers are a typical feature of the MiG-15.

The main wheel door of an early production MiG-15bis. The T-shaped antenna belongs to the RV-2 Kristal (Crystal) radio altimeter.

The main wheel wells of the MiG-15 contained a number of electrical and hydraulic lines. This is the starboard main wheel well.

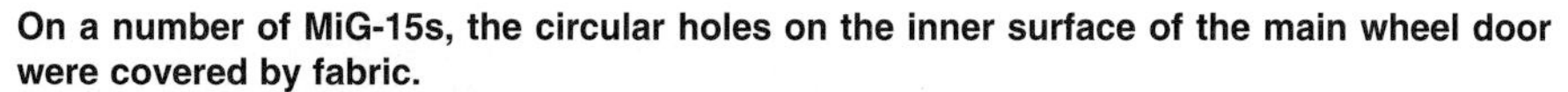

On a number of MiG-15s, the circular holes on the inner surface of the main wheel door were covered by fabric.

The LFSV-45 landing light was located on the port wing of Fagot-Bs that lacked the FS-155 landing light in the air intake splitter.

The starboard main landing gear of a Lim-2 Fagot-B. The main landing gear was equipped with oleo-pneumatic shock absorbers. The hoses are hydraulic lines for the brakes. The blister in front of the main wheel well is a radar warning receiver antenna, a device installed only on late service Polish Air Force Lim-2s.

The starboard main gear of a MiG-15. The hydraulic gear retraction system operated at a pressure of 140 bar (2,030 psi).

The Klimov VK-1 non afterburning engine of the MiG-15bis Fagot-B had an output of 2,700 kg (5,952 lb) thrust. The cutaway engine shows the the single stage centrifugal compressor with dual inlet ducts.

The front of a VK-1 engine once displayed in the Army Museum of the German Democratic Republic at Dresden. The gear box in the front of the compressor has been cut away to allow viewing of the compressor blades. When West Germany took possession of the museum, the VK-1 quickly disappeared.

The starboard side of a VK-1 engine with its nine straight-flow combustion chambers.

The starboard side of a VK-1 engine with the accessory gearbox for driving fuel, oil, and hydraulic pumps and electrical equipment. A screen was installed over the air intakes to avoid damage by foreign objects.

The VK-1 had a single-stage centrifugal compressor. The gears belong to the accessory gearbox. The compressor blades of this engine have been cut away for demonstration purposes.

For an overhaul of the VK-1 engine and its components, the entire rear portion of the fuselage could be removed.

The tail of this Polish Air Force Lim-2 Fagot-B has been removed with the help of a trolley. Most access panels on the rear fuselage are open. Each access hatch was connected to the fuselage with a wire to prevent its loss during maintenance. The latching mechanism of the circular hatch was copied from the World War II Messerschmitt Bf-109 fighter.

With its tail completely removed, this Polish Air Force Lim-2 Fagot-B is being pushed into a maintenance hangar. The PTB-260 slipper tanks and the rectangular shaped main wheel cover doors were unique features of the Fagot.

A two-seat MiG-15UTI undergoes an overhaul. The exhaust pipe has been removed from the engine.

This view up the exhaust pipe of an early MiG-15bis shows the turbine blades and the rear turbine bearing housing of the VK-1 turbojet engine.

The removed rear fuselage of a MiG-15bis reveals the details of its construction. The tube-shaped exhaust pipe was a typical feature of the VK-1 engine.

Both the Fagot-A and Fagot-B carried an EKSR-46 signal flare launcher on the starboard lower fuselage. Shown here is a Fagot-A.

On all MiG-15bis Fagot-Bs, the EKSR-46 signal flare launcher was relocated to a position slightly to the rear of and significantly higher than that of the Fagot-A.

The EKSR-46 signal flare launcher could be loaded with four flares of different colors, indicated by dots above the device. The EKSR-46 was a derivative of the German AZA-10 signal flare launcher system installed in the Messerschmitt Me 262. The device itself is not mounted in this particular MiG-15bis.

The rear starboard fuselage of a MiG-15bis Fagot-B with the SRO-1 Bariy-M IFF blade aerial. The small tube placed slightly in front of the engine access panel is the air pressure probe that was mounted only on the starboard side.

The rectangular fairing for the RPKO-10M radio compass on top of the fuselage identifies this aircraft as a MiG-15 Fagot-A. The air pressure probe above the engine access panel was installed on Fagot-As as well as Fagot-Bs.

A number of MiG-15 Fagot-As were retrofitted with an SRO-1 Bariy-M IFF aerial offset slightly to port. The rectangular covering for the RPKO-10M radio compass is visible in front of the SRO-1 antenna. This is a Czechoslovak-built MiG-15 in Romanian Air Force service.

The panel immediately behind the port wing root is for the external 20-volt power supply.

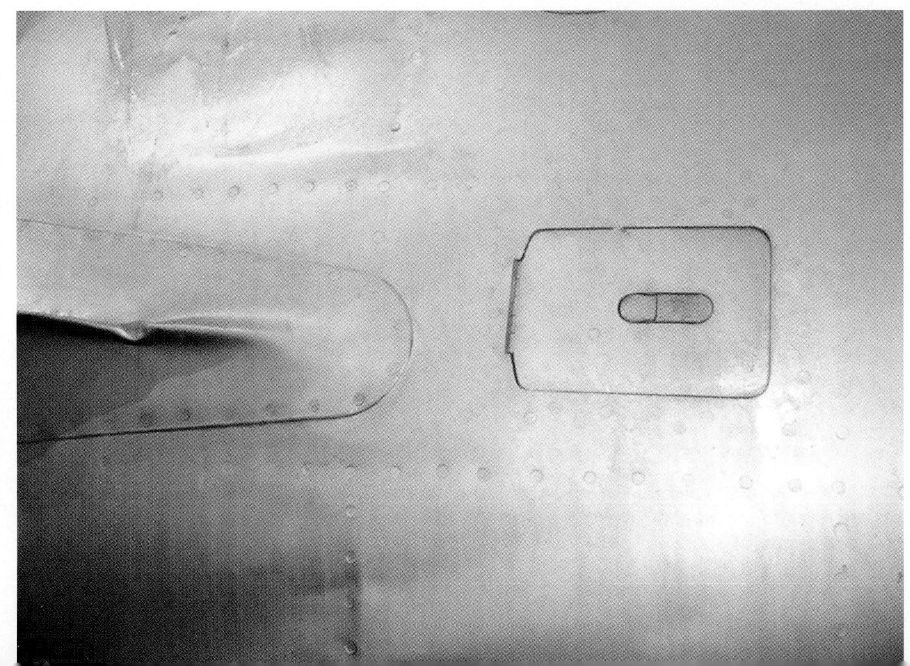

The open access hatch for the external power supply. The access panel for the 20-volt power supply of the MiG-15 was a snap-fit opening mechanism copied by the Soviet aircraft industry from the Messerschmitt Bf-109E-3 fighters that were supplied to the Soviet Union in 1940.

Engine Mount Variations

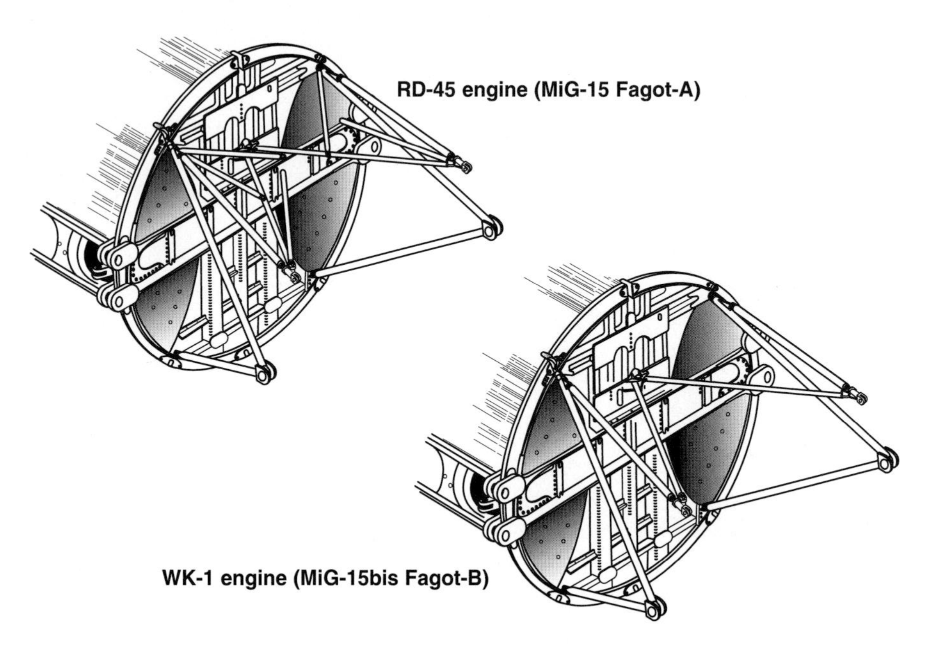

The main fuselage fuel filler cap was located behind the cockpit and slightly offset to port. The canopy fairing is visible on the left. The cap was identical throughout production of both the Mig-15 Fagot-A and the MiG-15bis Fagot-B. This fuel cap belongs to a Czechoslovak-built MiG-15bis.

The main fuel tank of this Polish built Lim-2 is being refilled. A fabric cover has been placed over the wing root to protect it during the refuelling procedure. The main fuel tank had a capacity of 1,250 liters (330 gal).

Maintenance on 'Red 65,' an Avia-built Bulgarian Air Force MiG-15 (serial number 231665). Most of the access panels have been removed from the rear fuselage. The rectangular dorsal fairing for the RPKO-10M radio compass as well the position of the EKSR-46 flare dispenser identifies this aircraft as a MiG-15 Fagot-A.

With the large circular access panel removed the ground crews could easily separate the tail from the forward fuselage.

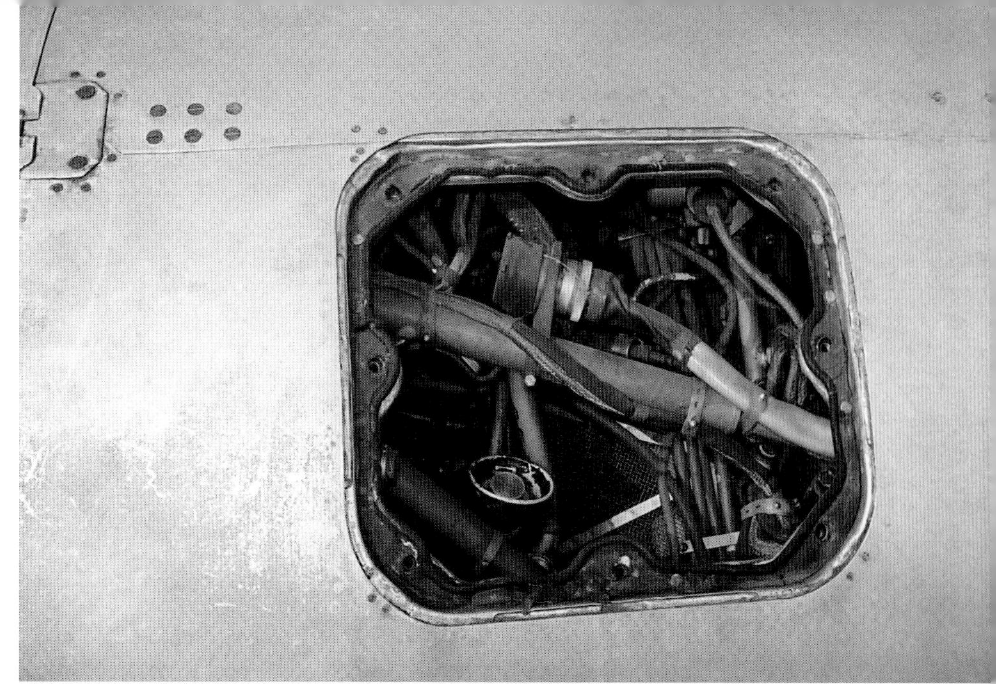

The rectangular access panel on the port rear fuselage. After this panel had been removed, the rear part of the fuselage could be easily separated from the rest of the aircraft. The access panels on both MiG-15 Fagot-A and MiG-15bis Fagot-B were identical.

The open access panels on the upper rear fuselage of an early production MiG-15bis of the Hungarian Air Force. The tube on the right is the air pressure probe.

The small speed brake of a Soviet-built MiG-15 Fagot-A in Polish Air Force service. Just in front of the speed brake are two circular panels.

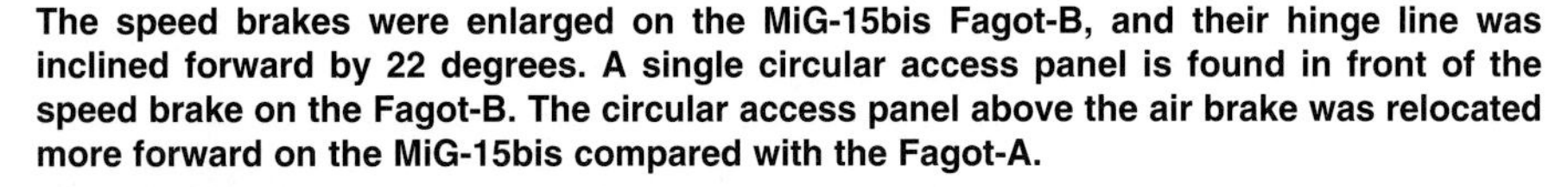

The speed brakes were enlarged on the MiG-15bis Fagot-B, and their hinge line was inclined forward by 22 degrees. A single circular access panel is found in front of the speed brake on the Fagot-B. The circular access panel above the air brake was relocated more forward on the MiG-15bis compared with the Fagot-A.

The port speed brake of a Polish MiG-15 Fagot-A. On the Fagot-A the speed brake hinge line was vertical, giving the airplane a tendency to pitch up when the brakes were deployed.

The jet pipe of the MiG-15bis' VK-1 engine was slightly extended, and as a result the contours of the aft fuselage were redesigned on the Fagot-B. The lower circular access hatch in front of the speed brake on the Fagot-A was relocated further forward on the Fagot-B. The speed brake is made of a single piece of stainless steel.

The speed brakes of early MiG-15bis Fagots were built of two pieces of sheet steel. The speed brakes were electro-hydraulically actuated and opened 55 degrees.

The tail of a Czechoslovak-built MiG-15bis Fagot-B. This particular aircraft is equipped with a one-piece stainless steel speed brake, a feature of late production Fagot-Bs. The majority of all MiG-15bis carried two-piece speed brakes.

Sheet metal reinforcements have been added to the vertical fin around the horizontal stabilizer of this MiG-15.

The attachment for the radio antenna on the vertical fin of a MiG-15. The MiG-15 Fagot-A and the MiG-15bis Fagot-B used an identical wire antenna.

Fuselage Underside Variations

MiG-15 Fagot-A

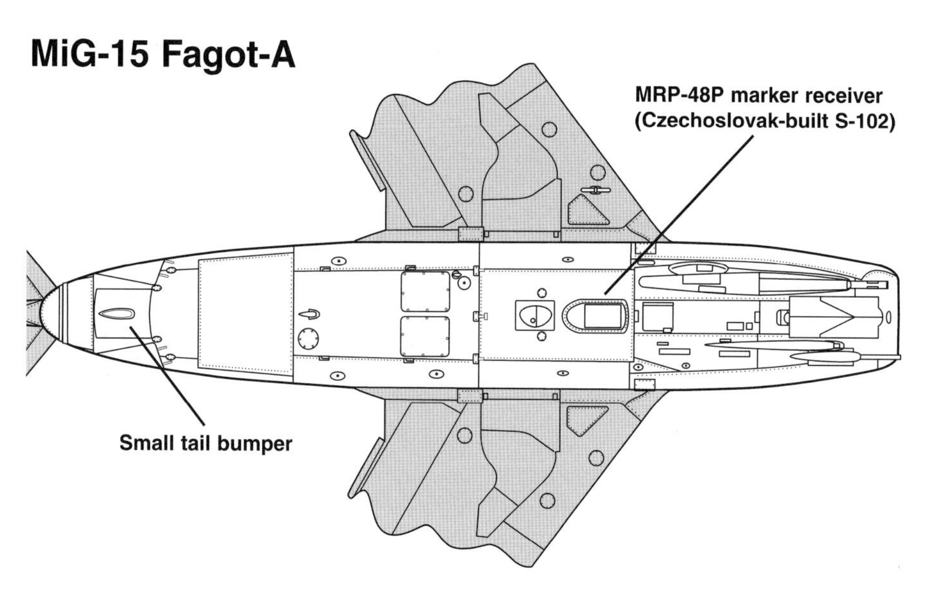

MiG-15bis Fagot-B

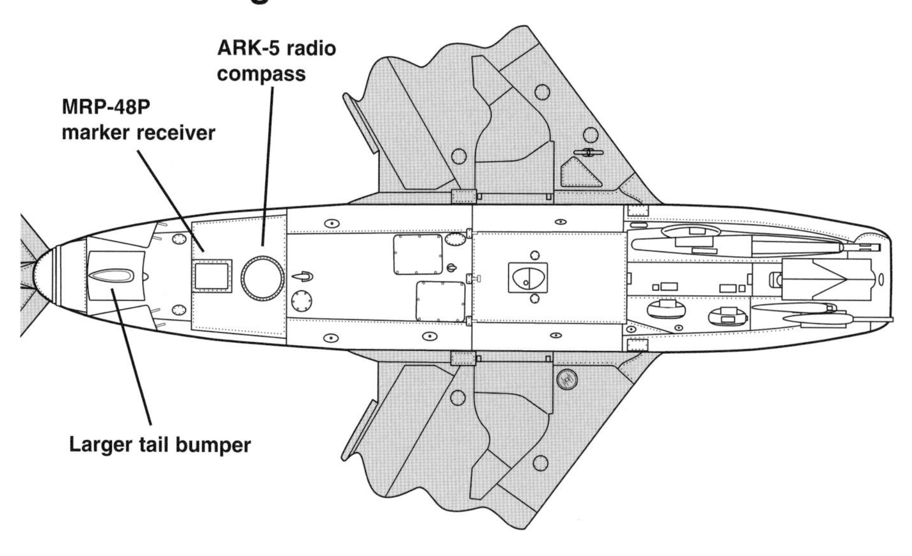

The cross-shaped tail of 'Red 1004,' a Polish Air Force Lim-2R (serial number 1B-010-04). The elevator trim tab is visible on the port elevator. The lorry is an external electrical power supply. Standard starting procedure for the MiG-15's VK-1 engine always called for a ground crewman standing at the nozzle observing the ignition and signalling the mechanic standing on the ladder close to the pilot.

Rear Fuselage Fuel Tank

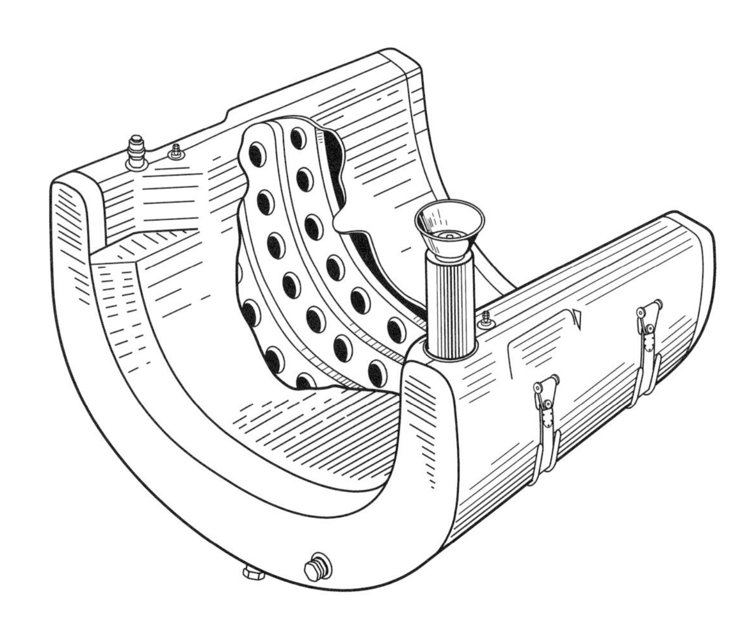

The antenna of the ARK-5 radio compass in the rear lower fuselage compartment with its transparent cover removed. The ARK-5 radio compass was a feature of all Fagot-Bs.

The panel on the starboard rear fuselage gives access to the servomotors. There was no corresponding panel on the port rear fuselage of the MiG-15bis.

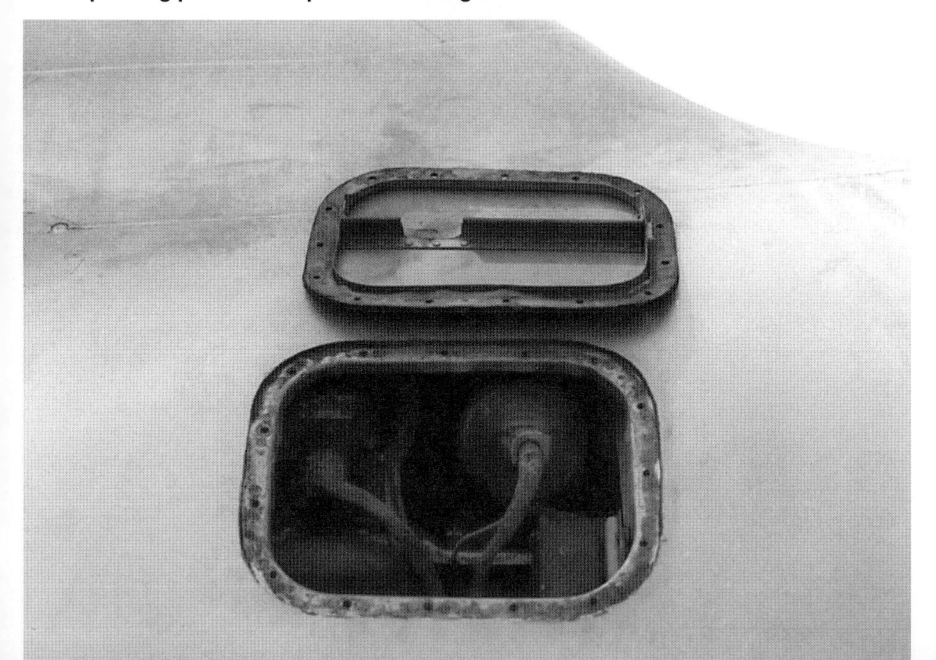

Even under the most austere winter conditions, the MiG-15 was easy to maintain. These Bulgarian ground crewmen are about to remove the tail of a MiG-15 Fagot-A from its fuselage with the help of cables. The tail section has been placed on a trolley. This particular Fagot-A has been retrofitted with an SRO-1 IFF blade aerial.

The port horizontal stabilizer of a Czechoslovak-built MiG-15bis. Only the port elevator had a trim tab, and the square access panel near the fin was found only on the port horizontal stabilizer.

The starboard horizontal stabilizer of the MiG-15 lacked an elevator trim tab as well as the square access panel. The position light is located on the fin fairing. Both elevators had a balance weight at the tip.

The port elevator with the trim tab and the fairing covering the trim tab control mechanism. This fairing was only found on the lower surface. Externally, there was no difference between the Fagot-A and Fagot-B stabilizer during the production cycle.

The balance weight of the port elevator. In contrast to the Czechoslovak-built aircraft, the edges of the hinge reinforcement panel were less pointed on Polish built MiG-15s.

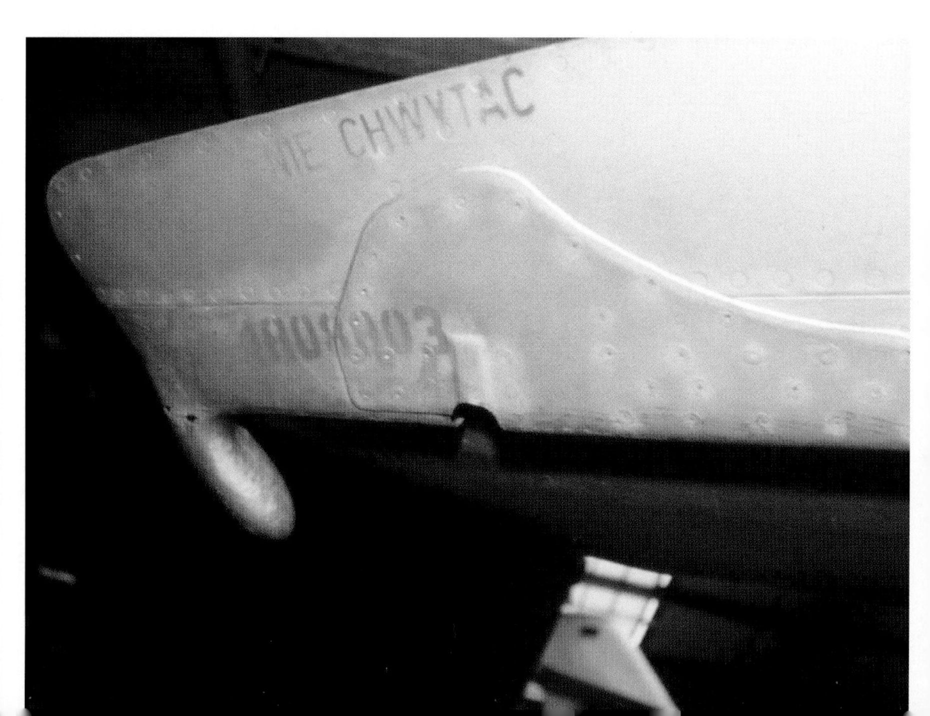

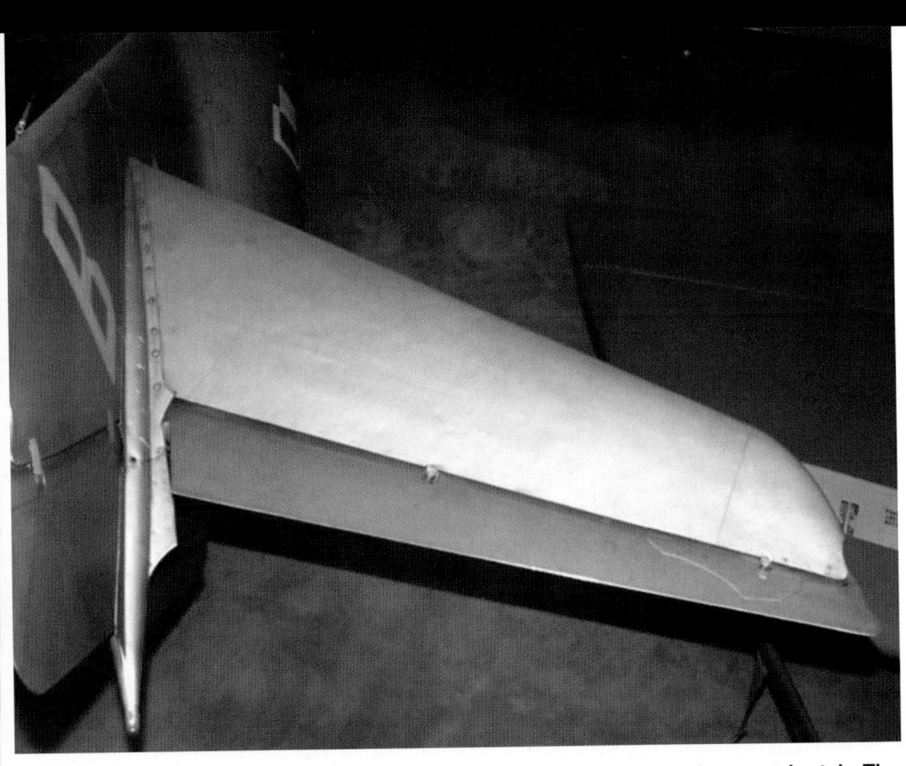

The starboard horizontal stabilizer viewed from above. The elevator has no trim tab. The horizontal stabilizers of the MiG-15 single- and two-seater were identical.

The port horizontal stabilizer, elevator, and elevator trim tab viewed from above. There is no hinge control mechanism on the upper surface of the trim tab.

The rear position light of a MiG-15. This device was identical on MiG-15 single- and two-seaters.

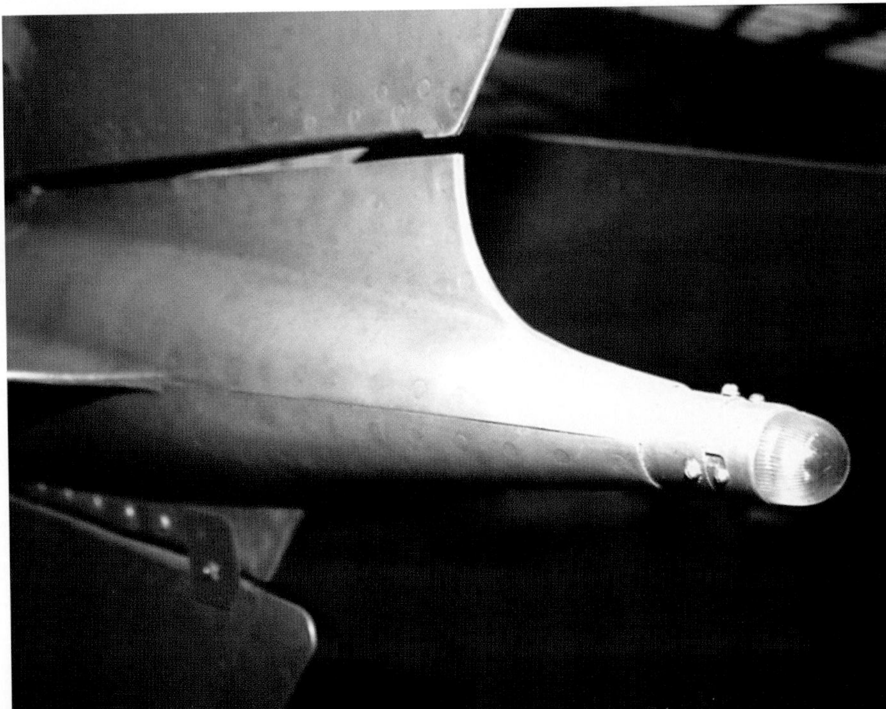

The tip of the vertical fin and rudder viewed from above. Both elevators and the rudder of all versions of the MiG-15 were equipped with balance weights.

The fully extended speed brakes of an engineless MiG-15 Fagot-A. This Fagot-A previously saw service with the Czechoslovak Air Force before it was retired at Olomouc-Holice airfield in August 1958.

The horizontal stabilizer removed from a MiG-15bis of the Hungarian Air Force. For transportation of the MiG-15 by road, wings and horizontal stabilizers could be easily removed.

The vertical fin of a MiG-15bis with the upper tail and the horizontal stabilizer removed. Part of the fairing above the engine nozzle also has been removed, as well as most of the access hatches.

All access hatches and fuel tank filler caps on the rear fuselage of this particular MiG-15bis have been removed. The locking mechanism of the circular rear fuel tank filler caps was copied from the German Messerschmitt Bf-109G fighter.

Antenna Variations

MiG-15 Fagot-A/MiG-15bis Fagot-B (early)

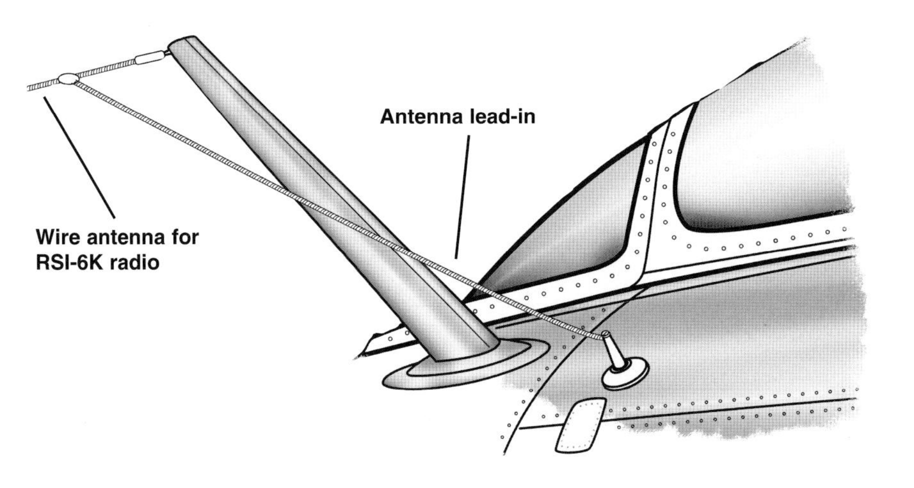

MiG-15bis Fagot-B (late)

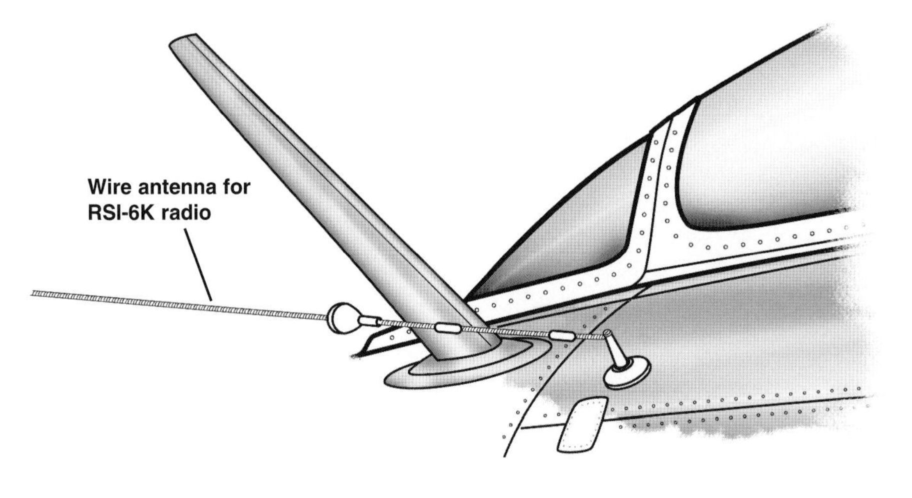

A MiG-15bis Fagot-B of the Bulgarian Air Force being readied for a mission. This Fagot-B is equipped with a one-piece stainless steel speed brake. The position of the national marking at the top of the vertical fin is unique to the Bulgarian Air Force.

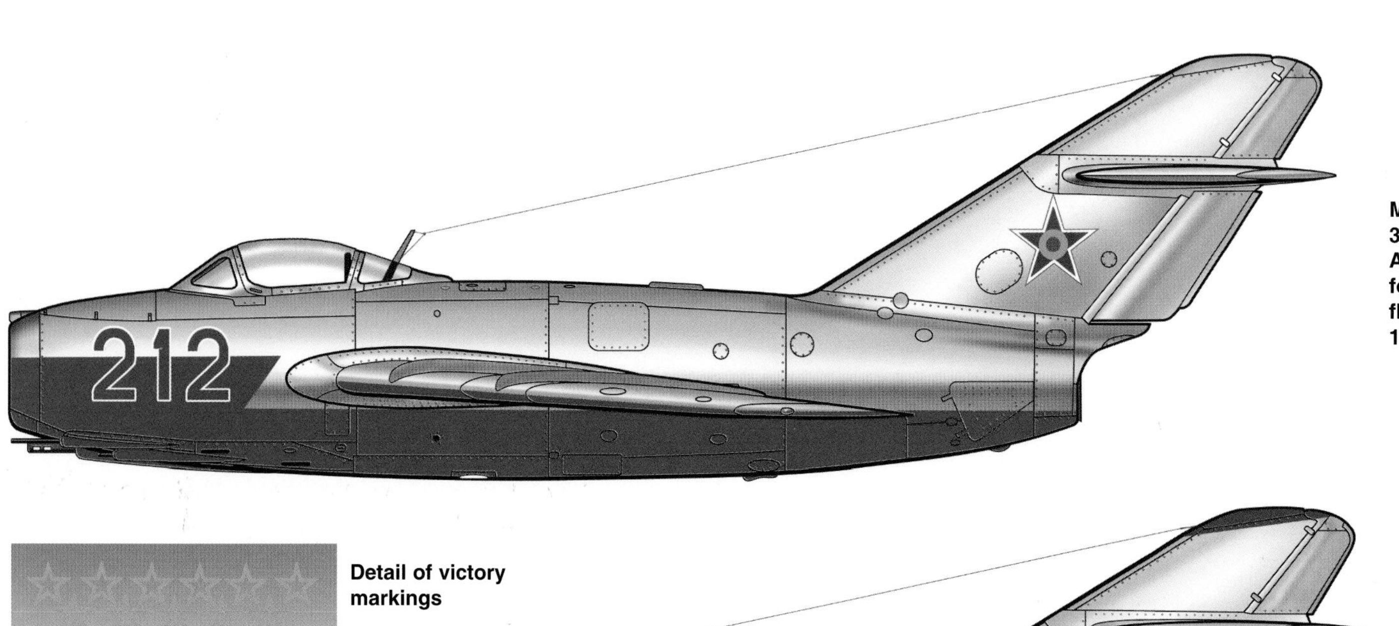

MiG-15 Fagot-A 'Red 212' (serial number 3810212), 62nd Fighter Wing, Hungarian Air Force, Kecskemet Air Base, 1954. A former Soviet Air Force aircraft, 'Red 212' flew in Hungarian service from 1951 to 1957, when it was returned to the USSR.

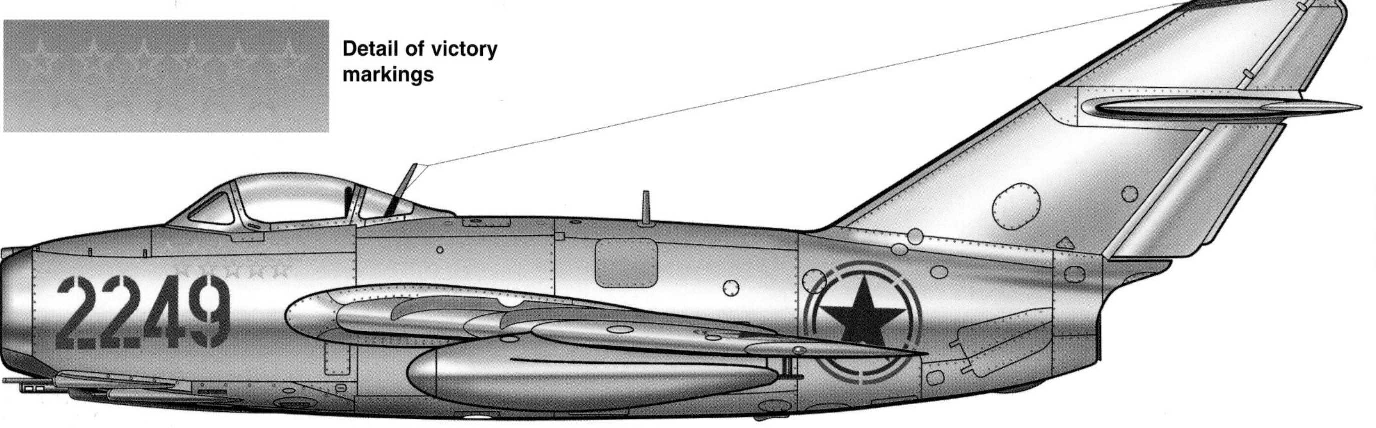

MiG-15bis Fagot-B 'Red 2249' of the North Korean Air Force piloted by Flying Officer Wan-Hai, Commander, 7th Chinese Fighter Wing, Manchuria, 1953.

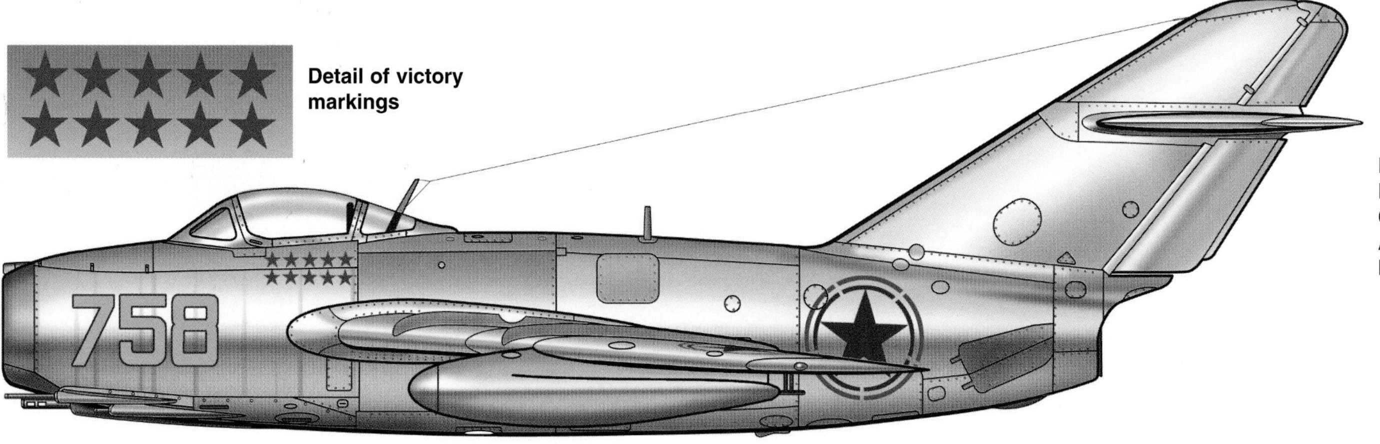

MiG-15bis Fagot-B 'Yellow 758' of the North Korean Air Force flown by Russian Captain Pavel Milauszkin, 176 Fighter Aviation Regiment, 324 Fighter Aviation Division, 1952.

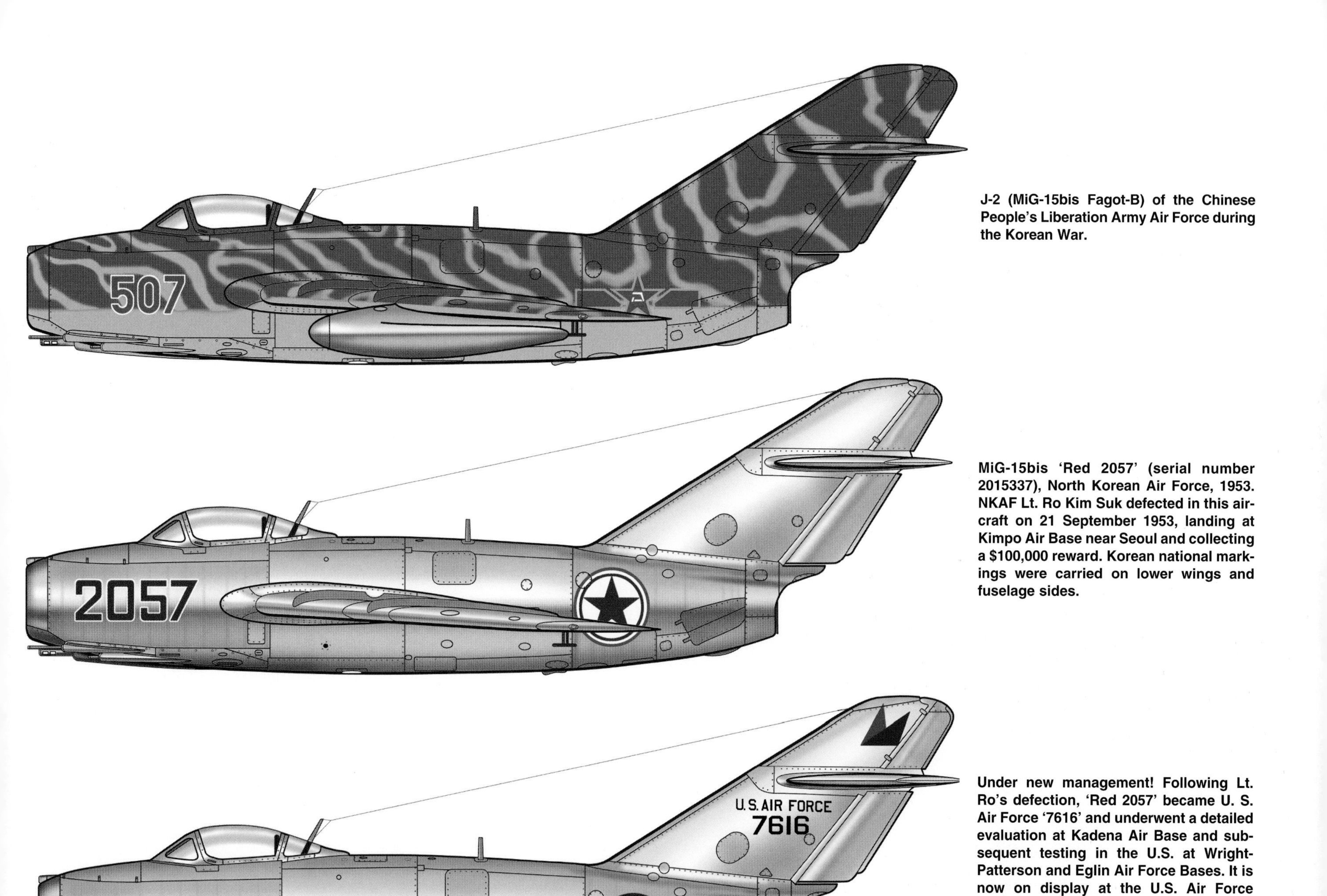

J-2 (MiG-15bis Fagot-B) of the Chinese People's Liberation Army Air Force during the Korean War.

MiG-15bis 'Red 2057' (serial number 2015337), North Korean Air Force, 1953. NKAF Lt. Ro Kim Suk defected in this aircraft on 21 September 1953, landing at Kimpo Air Base near Seoul and collecting a $100,000 reward. Korean national markings were carried on lower wings and fuselage sides.

Under new management! Following Lt. Ro's defection, 'Red 2057' became U. S. Air Force '7616' and underwent a detailed evaluation at Kadena Air Base and subsequent testing in the U.S. at Wright-Patterson and Eglin Air Force Bases. It is now on display at the U.S. Air Force Museum, Dayton, Ohio.

'Red 165,' a Bulgarian MiG-15 Fagot-A, gets a tow from a Soviet Jeep. The tactical number had been given a thin black outline. This Fagot-A was equipped with a SRO-1 IFF blade aerial. The position of the EKSR-46 flare dispenser on the lower part of the rear fuselage identifies this aircraft as a Fagot-A.

'Red 850,' a Soviet Air Force MiG-15bis (serial number 53210850) assigned to the Flight Research Institute. The last three digits of the serial number had been repeated as tactical number. This Fagot-B was manufactured by the State Aircraft Factory 21 at Gorky.

'Red 040,' a Bulgarian Air Force MiG-15bis gets a tow. Most Bulgarian Fagot-Bs were delivered from the Soviet Union; an additional 15 MiG-15s were purchased in 1955 from Aero in Czechoslovakia.

Two Polish Air Force Lim-2 Fagot-Bs being readied for a training mission. 'Red 314' (serial number 1B-003-14) has part of its upper rear fuselage painted in red.

(Above) 'Red 48' after a few years' service The aluminum finish is no longer as shiny as in the photo at left. The hammer and circle emblem in the East German national markings indicates that the photo was taken after late 1959. In the meantime the tactical number has been fully painted on and PTB-260 slipper tanks added on the wing.

(Above) 'Red 48,' a brand new Czechoslovak-built MiG-15bis of the Luftstreitkräfte der Nationalen Volksarmee (East German Air Force). This is a very late production Fagot-B with the late-style nose wheel that became standard on all MiG-17s. The first MiG-15bis were allocated to the East German Air Force in June 1956, a total of 30 Aero-built Fagot-Bs being delivered. This style of national marking was carried between 1956 and autumn 1959. The tactical number is stenciled.

(Right) 'Red 16,' a late Soviet-built Fagot-B (serial number 1768) of the East German Air Force equipped with PTB-400 drop tanks.

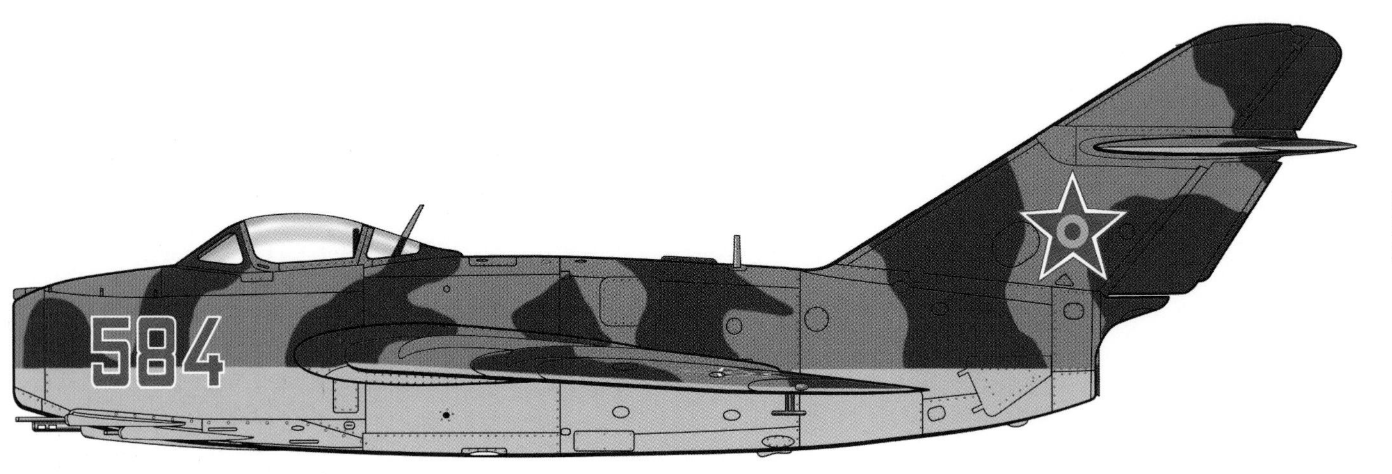

MiG-15 Fagot-A 'Red 584,' Romanian Air Force, in Earth Brown and Olive Drab ground attack camouflage.

MiG-15 Fagot-A '1303' target exercise aircraft, Czechoslovak Air Force, early 1960s.

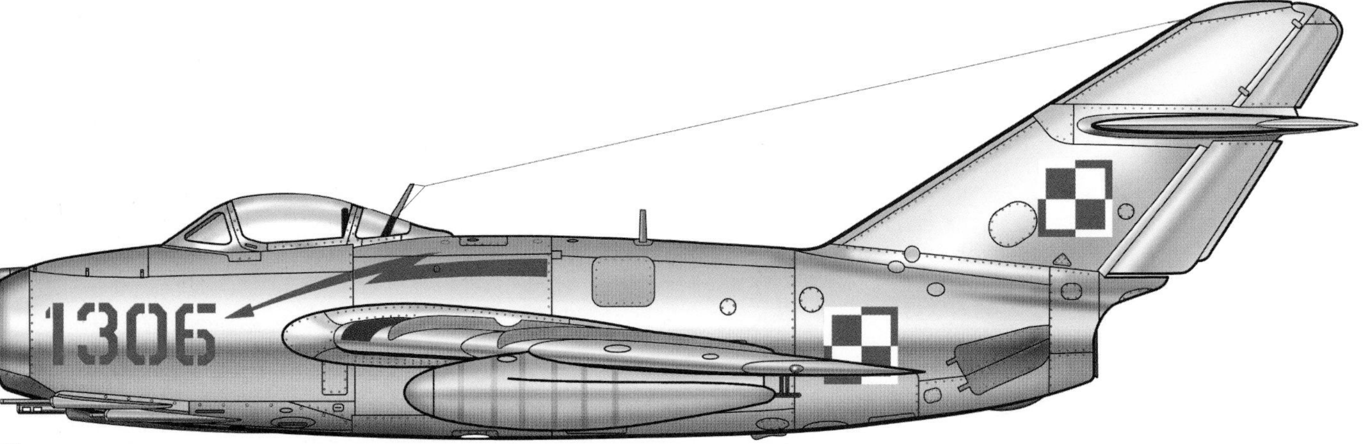

Lim-2 (Polish-built MiG-15) 'Red 1306' (serial Number 1B01012) of the 1st Fighter Regiment "Warszawa," Polish Air Force, Minsk Mazowiecki Air Base, 1959. The red lightning arrow denotes an award for crew excellence.

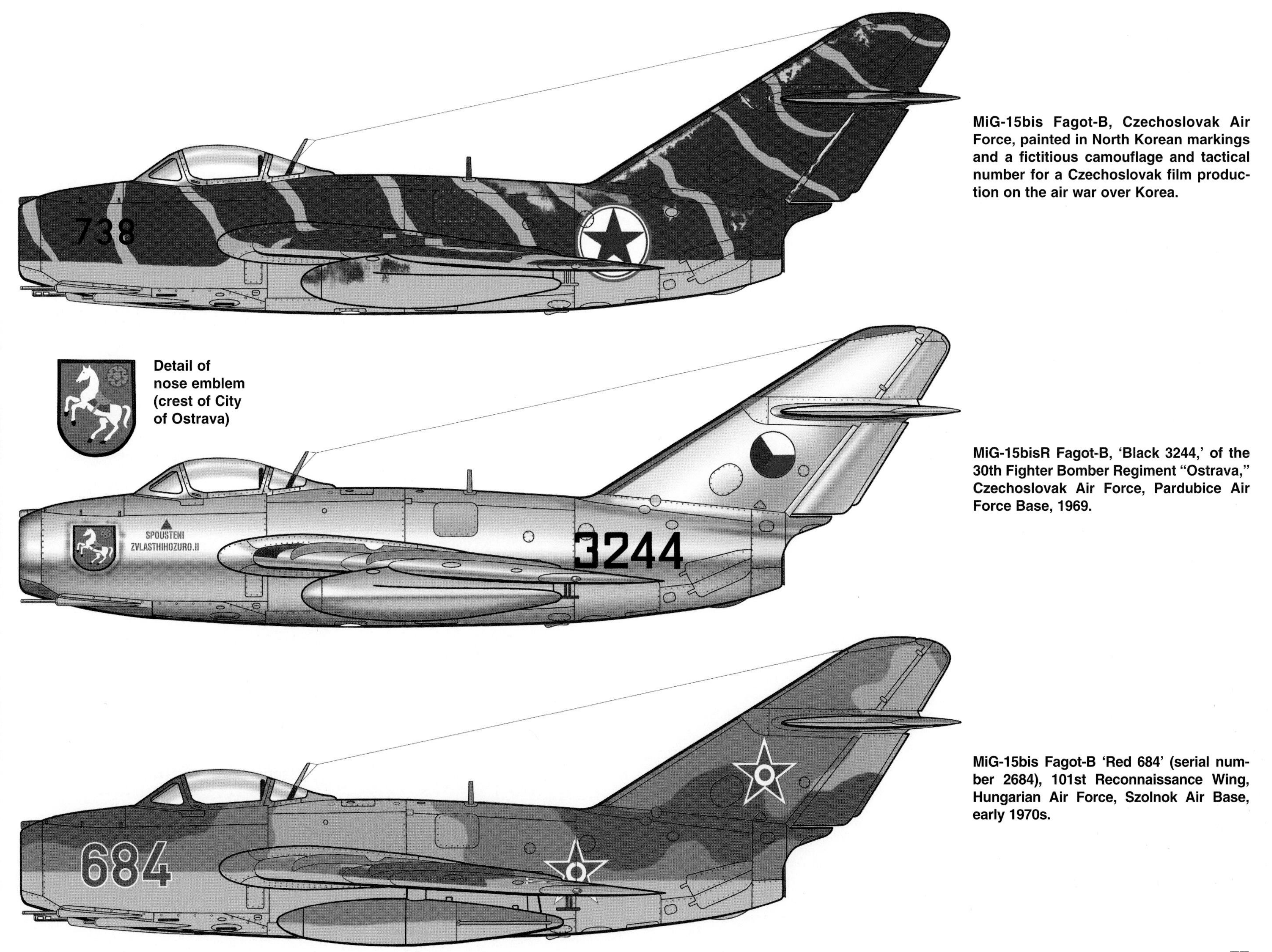

MiG-15bis Fagot-B, Czechoslovak Air Force, painted in North Korean markings and a fictitious camouflage and tactical number for a Czechoslovak film production on the air war over Korea.

Detail of nose emblem (crest of City of Ostrava)

MiG-15bisR Fagot-B, 'Black 3244,' of the 30th Fighter Bomber Regiment "Ostrava," Czechoslovak Air Force, Pardubice Air Force Base, 1969.

MiG-15bis Fagot-B 'Red 684' (serial number 2684), 101st Reconnaissance Wing, Hungarian Air Force, Szolnok Air Base, early 1970s.

This Hungarian MiG-15bis, 'Red 902,' (serial number 31530902) was built at State Aircraft Factory 31 at Tbilisi. The tail marking, a black triangle with a black letter 'C' denotes the 50th Fighter Aviation Regiment. The tactical number 'Red 902' has a thin white outline. All Hungarian Air Force MiG-15s were built in the Soviet Union.

A MiG-15bis of the Czechoslovak Air Force being readied during a winter exercise. During summer 1957 the four-digit tactical marking applied to the nose was replaced by a four-digit marking painted on the rear fuselage. In September 1956 the Czechoslovak designation 'S-103' was changed to the original 'MiG-15bis.'

This late production MiG-15bis, 'Red 060' of the 101st Reconnaissance Aviation Wing, Hungarian Air Force. A brown and green camouflage was applied on the upper surfaces. The lower surfaces were painted in light blue, and the tactical number was outlined in white. The aircraft had previously served as an interceptor in overall natural metal finish.

A freshly completed S-103 during acceptance procedures for the Czechoslovak Air Force. Note the digit '2' and the winged star emblem in the air intake splitter as well as the factory number '38' applied on the nose. A total of 620 S-103s (MiG-15bis) were manufactured for the Czechoslovak Air Force by Aero.

Senior Lieutenant Ro Kim Suk defected with this MiG-15bis 'Red 2057' (serial number 2015337) to Kimpo Air Base near Seoul on 21st September 1953. The red star and the red and blue circles had been painted against the natural silver.

'Red 2057' was an early production Fagot-B built by State Aircraft Factory 153 at Novosibirsk. It still had the FS-155 landing light installed in the air intake splitter and carried the early antenna cable configuration like that of the Fagot-A.

The former North Korean MiG-15bis 'Red 2057' during evaluation trials at Wright-Patterson Air Force Base, Dayton, Ohio. The "TC" in front of the 'buzz' number reputedly were the initials of U.S. Air Force test pilot Major Harold E. "Tom" Collins, who previously in November 1953 had flown a former Albanian Air Force Yak-23 'Flora' (USAF registration FU-559) that the United States received thru clandestine channels from Yugoslavia.